CLEAR YOUR HEAD TO GET AHEAD

THE ANTIDOTE TO STRESS

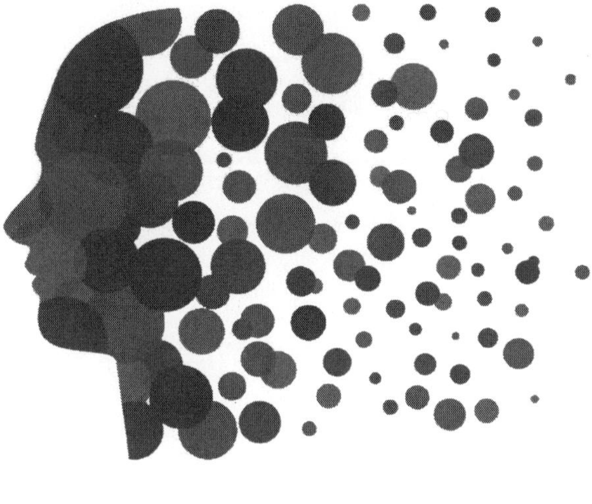

MARTIN DAUBNEY

Martin Daubney
Inspire Coaching GmbH
Riehenstrasse 64, Basel, Switzerland
www.Martin-Daubney.com

For Fiona
1964 – 2019

TABLE OF CONTENTS

Introduction

Look around any book shop in any town or airport in the world, and there will be a section headed Self Help. This is where you will find answers to your current dilemma, learn how to cope with your fears and phobias, or find out how to handle stress. You may even have found this book there...either there or in the special offer section.

Unfortunately, this section is often neglected by the people who could probably use it the most, those people who struggle with their workload, overwhelm, and being overloaded, leading them on the dark path towards anxiety, depression, and burnout. The trouble is, it's not as easy as that. Most of the experiences described in this book seemingly just happen to people. Most people really do not recognise the signs that depression and anxiety are looming any more than they would recognise the feeling of what it's like to sit in a chair until their attention is brought to it. Denial played a huge role in the stories of the people in this book as much as the belief that "it won't happen to me". Sadly, it did and continues to do so for them and many others.

The real motivation for writing this, though, comes from life experiences, my clients' as well as my own. I was in a coaching conversation figuring out how a client reached their anxiety, and they suddenly let slip a key piece of information. This often happens, and to the client, it seems quite ordinary, but for the coach, it's often the gem that leads to profound change for the client. On this occasion, the client casually let me know that in times of very high workload and work pressure, they simply "slip a Benzo". Now, forgive me, but not being in the high-pressure workplace of a corporate environment, I had no idea what a Benzo was. Turns out it's short for "benzodiazepine", a class of drugs that includes, among others, Valium. I must admit I was a little shocked and not prepared for what followed. The client then went on to say, "it's OK, we all do it. Sometimes people ask which Benzo are you on to check for efficacy". There is, it seems, an open drug culture raging through the offices of global corporations just so that people working in these companies can do their jobs. That didn't sit well with me, so *Clear Your Head to Get Ahead* was born. I suppose it could also be called, "How to be able to do your job without the need for drugs to take away the stress", but that's not so snappy!

As you continue through this book, I will share some of the most effective and powerful techniques I have been taught and studied to give you the best current thinking on how to manage your stress. I will also illustrate them with real people's stories who were, at the time, unable to reconcile their experiences with the early stages of burnout, leading them into a full-blown breakdown and everything that goes with it.

What isn't going to happen is me letting you into a secret world where there is no stress, an impossible utopia. If you find that disappointing, I'm pleased to have got that out of the way nice and early, so you can settle back and read on with confidence, knowing that you'll probably learn something, have plenty to think about, and won't be lied to.

Enjoy.

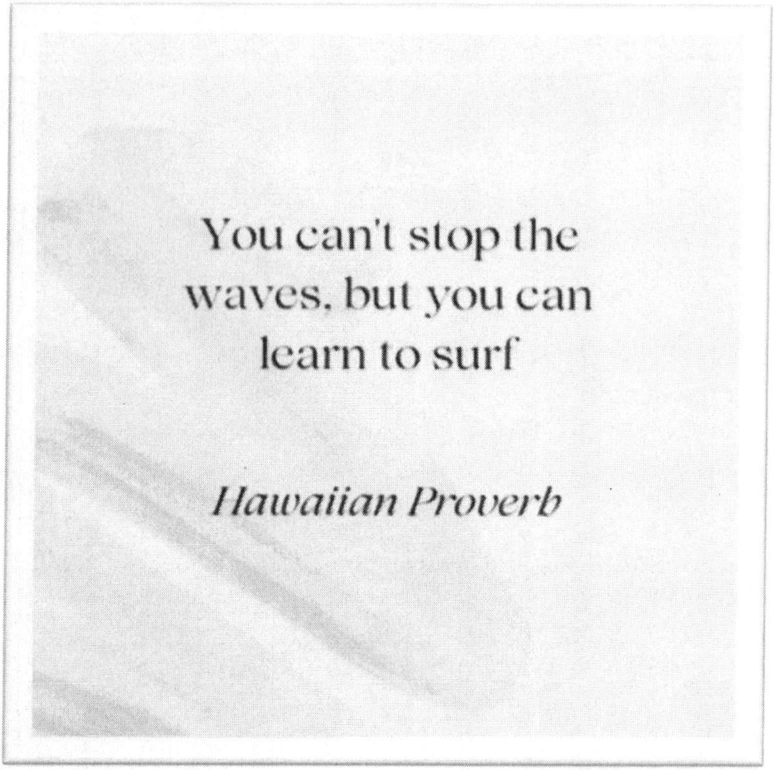
You can't stop the
waves, but you can
learn to surf
Hawaiian Proverb

CHAPTER 1

It Won't Happen to Me

It is truly a symptom of our time that wherever you go and whoever you talk to, one topic will always come up; how busy we are. It's almost a badge of honour to let everyone know how busy you are. In fact, if you are not busy at all, or maybe even stressed, what on earth are you doing? What most people don't understand is there is a vast difference between activity and progress, and progress doesn't always need a show of business. Most people do recognise that they are overbusy. Although some brave souls will push back on their line managers when they are requested to take on more, most people fail to see that there is a marked difference between being busy, i.e., doing stuff, and progress, i.e., doing specific tasks that take you towards your goal. You've probably seen busy people where you work. You can spot them as they tend to always carry something like a notebook and pen, or maybe a folio or some folders. They are almost always in a meeting, coming back from a meeting, or just about to head off into another meeting.

Oh...meetings! That's another chapter!

So, what's all this about clearing your head? Well, it's all to do with how we make what sense we can of the world outside us. You know that thing when people tell you, "Yeah... well, in the real world," or maybe, "That's OK in your model of the world". There is some truth in this. It's one of the things that we are constantly working out, how to make sense of the world. And we all do it with a different understanding of how to get on in life. All creatures have a sense of what's safe and not safe in their environment, to some extent. In mammals, and in humans specifically, this is the job of the most primitive part of our rather clunky brain, the reptilian brain or brain stem. This is the first part of the human brain to mature and the only part of our brain that is fully functioning at birth. It's the part that controls our breathing, heart rate, balance, and temperature and is on constant alert for our safety. So, if the fabled sabre-toothed tiger was to suddenly jump out of the bushes towards you, your reptilian brain would do all it could to get you out of the way and quickly.

These days, though, there's a serious absence of sabre-toothed tigers, although there are plenty of other things around us to trigger the same response, and for most people in an office or sedentary based job, that can be the start of the problem. Back in the days of the tiger, if you saw one, you'd be able to run like crazy to get to safety. These days the role of the tiger has been taken over by the boss, another car driver, or an infuriating neighbour or colleague, so when we get the "attack", we are seated and not necessarily able to move physically out of the way. The trouble with this scenario is that when we are "attacked", our stress hormone, cortisol, rises in our bloodstream. It's one of the things that help us get out of the way, and one of the quickest ways to lower the level of cortisol is movement, fast movement too. So, if you do happen to have had a verbal lashing from your boss, or they have looked at you in an odd way, your cortisol levels rise and sit with you for hours. This is not good news and not good for your body which must deal with all the negative consequences of high cortisol.

We do need some cortisol, don't get me wrong, but a high, sustained level will lead to all the negative symptoms of too much stress, including high blood pressure, increased anxiety, and a higher susceptibility to infections. So, it's probably a good idea to be in control when the tiger attacks!

That's all very well, but what's this got to do with clearing my head, and clearing of what... exactly? You can only make sense of what is going on based on the thoughts you generate inside your head. Mostly, you delete information that you consider to be of no help to your survival with no direct impact on you. For example, it is possible to delete all external noises in a crowded room so you can focus on listening to just one person. Or you can delete the sensations of what your feet feel like right now, except that now I've drawn your attention to them, you will feel them.

The process of deletion can be quite automatic and offers us hope for focused attention in this world of too much distraction. Deletion reduces the world to proportions which we feel capable of handling. Just put yourself in a crowded room, for example, and hone in on the one conversation you want to be part of. It can be done, but in so doing, you are deleting all the other information being shared by others in the room. This may be useful in some contexts yet be the source of pain in others. Our attention is selective, so be careful what you focus on.

We also distort information. In this process, we accept information into our sensory system, play around with it for a microsecond so we can make sense of what just happened, and in so doing, we distort it. The chances are if we replay the information we receive as a message, we will pass on our distortion of that information only for it to be distorted again by the receiver. However, this is not necessarily bad news, as through our distortion, we often create, manufacture, manipulate, and even construct new sensory information. Distortion is the process that allows us to make shifts in our experience of sensory data. For example, fantasy and artistic creativity, along with all the revolutionary discoveries of the sciences, come from our ability to distort. We distort what we hear, see, feel, taste, and smell, so it more comfortably fits with our model of the world, our values, and our beliefs.

Sometimes, we might misrepresent our reality by distorting our experience of pure sensory information. This sort of behaviour probably started when we were children, perhaps remembering the first time we were caught doing something we probably shouldn't have been doing and not wanting to admit it to our elders. Being intimidated by certain people, frightened of a harmless situation, procrastinating, or misinterpreting what someone says, are examples of how we can distort reality. The process of planning, imagining, or visualising something also uses distortion, but this time as a way of constructing goals and compelling futures or building the Star Wars franchise.

The process of learning and drawing conclusions so that information can be applied for the achievement of any task needs to generalise that information and clump it together in our memory filing cabinet. A toddler who learns how to open a door for the first time quickly generalises their new ability so that all types of doors can be opened in a very similar way. Similarly, a negative experience may generalise through a person's life and result in issues later, e.g., being bitten once by a dog can result in a phobia of dogs. The person generalises that all dogs are dangerous because of the one-time event. These life experiences get grouped so that when we see something similar, we can apply similar knowledge to whatever it is we see.

The challenge for adults, though, is keeping an open mind so that the learning doesn't stop. If we stop learning, we stop growing and start dying. While it's OK to tell ourselves that the situation we find ourselves in now might be like something we have seen before, we can't predict the outcome. So, however stressful it may be, what we do with that stress will have a bearing on what happens next.

We have all felt the impacts of stress at some point in our lives, whether it be our life or the lives of those around us. From work deadlines to school assignments or even paying the bills, stress crops up in many different aspects of our lives. Short-term stress can make us feel anxious, exhausted, and irritable but is sometimes necessary for productivity and accomplishing our goals. However, chronic stress can have serious impacts on our health and well-being, which can ultimately lead to a shorter life span.

Long-term stress is proven to have negative effects on our health and is much more common than one would imagine. According to WebMD, around 33 per cent of people report feeling repeated and extreme stress in their daily lives. The causes of chronic stress can be anything from financial problems to a high-pressure job to issues with family or our relationships. Stress directly impacts our health in various ways, especially over the long term.

There are many indicators that a person may be experiencing chronic stress. If they are overwhelmed and constantly busy, it may not be that easy for them to identify the symptoms and admit they are stress-related.

One of the most common symptoms of chronic stress is frequent tension headaches. These can occur because, when under stress, you are probably not supplying your mind with as much oxygen as it needs. The build-up of emotions that stress brings to our minds increases muscle tension and can impact our sleep. Stress can also increase our general anxiety levels, leaving us on edge and irritable throughout the day. Stress-related anxiety causes rapid breathing, high blood pressure, frequent stomach aches, and a weakened immune system. These impacts on your body leave you at risk of heart attacks and potentially very serious diseases.

According to the American Institute of Stress, it is not the stressful situations but how you deal with the stress that affects your health and can kill you. When your stress is excessive over long periods of time, you will begin to experience the above symptoms and have a high risk of anxiety, depression, and even suicidal thoughts.

A study done by the Mental Health Foundation discovered that 32 per cent of respondents who were experiencing chronic stress admitted to having some form of suicidal thoughts at some point in their lives. Heart disease is another common way that stress impacts the body. People often turn to excessive eating, drugs, or alcohol to manage chronic stress, but this worsens their symptoms and long-term health. The high blood pressure and cholesterol that result from these decisions can damage the artery walls and eventually lead to life-threatening heart problems.

Fortunately, there are many ways to overcome chronic stress and prevent it from having lasting impacts on your health. One of the best ways to manage stress is to stay away from alcohol, drugs, and caffeine.

Having a set daily routine allows the body to feel less stressed and overwhelmed with responsibilities. This can also allow you to maintain a healthy lifestyle and make time for exercise each day, even if it means waking up an hour earlier. Routines also help with maintaining a good sleep pattern and getting the proper amounts of sleep each night. You will experience fewer problems falling asleep if you go to bed at the same time each night, and your body will get adjusted to waking up early in the morning after a restful night's sleep.

There are many ways to manage stress and overcome it to prevent the life-threatening impacts that stress can have on the body and your overall health. It is important to take the necessary steps to avoid these problems and stay mentally and physically healthy for the long term.

We live in a vibrational universe. Our thoughts and feelings are vibrations that are constantly shaping our world. Choose to vibrate LOVE.

CHAPTER 2

A Deer Knows It's a Deer

A few years ago, I heard a story about a shaman in Honduras who taught an extremely useful technique to dissolve stress and anxiety. Here it is for you.

Like much of the healing wisdom that comes from native cultures, this teaching began with an observation about nature. Sitting together, the shaman asked his class how they felt about deer. Yes, our furry four-legged friend that frolics in the forest. He explained that it is a mighty power animal and a great role model for us humans to learn from.

"A deer knows it's a deer. It has no inner conflict about its past, purpose, needs, or destiny. It lives in the moment and is always 100% resourceful, minute by minute; its senses are completely keen, and its focus is pure and unburdened."

Can you say that you spend most of your day this way? Or even just an hour? Some might argue this is not even possible in today's world. However, while we may not be able to live with completely clear and open minds like our furry counterparts, we

CAN begin to nurture longer stretches of this purity in our lives.

How do we do this?

An ancient technique:

The practice below is all about noticing and preventing yourself from being derailed either mentally or emotionally. What do I mean by the word "derailed"? I'm talking about allowing yourself to be distracted by thoughts that aren't serving you.

For example, you wake up and are having a beautiful morning until you catch a glimpse of yourself in the mirror and notice something you don't like. "Wow, I'm getting… (fill in the blank with your personal peeve– old, fat, skinny, bald, ugly, pale, stupid etc.)".

This is the bright shiny detour sign that beckons you to stop travelling your peaceful path and start engaging in negative self-analysis. Mostly we don't even notice this road sign; we just drive right off the highway into the valley of the downward spiral.

This might be a five- to ten-minute dialogue with yourself laden with low thoughts that sap your energy for an hour and sometimes for the entire day.

The mirror is just one example, but it could be a phone call, a text message, a minor inconvenience that triggers a stress response, or just the product of over-thinking your life with a busy brain instead of simply being in the moment.

There are so many ways to get there, but the destination is the same.

Derailed.

As you work with them, you begin to see these mental detours for what they truly are, invisible bars of a cage imprisoning your true self. Here is how I was taught to address these sneaky pitfalls and break the chains.

1. Pick an hour in your day. It doesn't need to be quiet or free of distraction. This practice is best done as part of your everyday life. You can be at work, with family, doing household chores, out for a hike, etc. The only thing that matters is that you start this hour in a positive and happy frame of mind.

2. All I want you to do is proceed through life over the next 60 minutes remaining as peaceful as you can. The only work you need to do is pay attention to your thoughts and gently note whenever you find yourself slipping into negative self-talk or getting derailed. This derailing doesn't need to be major for it to qualify; it can be as subtle as a two-second judgement or moment of anxiety.

To be clear, this practice is not about working with your negative thought pattern. You are simply taking inventory of what comes up in your periphery over the course of an hour of daily life. The more emotionally neutral you can be, the more information you will pick up.

The shaman gave me this bit of wisdom before I started: "We are watching our thoughts like a child on a riverbank notices what floats by. Curious, playful even, but unattached".

You might want to write these negative triggers down so that they can be worked with later, but this is completely your choice. This life habit has helped me in two key ways:

- The points of disruption as we walk through life are great entryways or portals into deeper inner work LATER.

- The simple act of observing and acknowledging your triggers with an open and neutral eye can bring healing to them in ways that your brain cannot quantify. The light of consciousness is healing in itself.

If you're up for it, I'd like to challenge you to do one of these power hours of self-discovery. Anyone can do it, and the benefits to body and soul can be extraordinary. Yes, it's work, but it's some of the most rewarding work I know. Are you with me?

Adapted from Nick Polizzi, founder of the Sacred Science.

Life is not about how fast you run or how high you climb but how well you bounce.

Vivian Komori

CHAPTER 3

Stress Makes You Sick

One thing we all know about stress is that too much of the bad sort will make you sick. The negative effects of stress are directly associated with several health issues, including problems with the immune system, digestion, anxiety, muddled thinking, and cardiovascular problems, most notably cardiac arrest. I don't know about you, but I know several people who categorically know that being overly stressed for a prolonged period was the thing that led to their breakdown, collapse, or car accident. The thing is, while these people may believe that the root cause of their life-changing event was stress, it has more to do with their beliefs, and, in particular, their belief about stress.

In 2013, health psychologist Kelly McGonigal gave a TED talk to raise public awareness of a study from the University of Wisconsin-Madison. The premise was that the researchers took a good look at some 1998 survey data conducted by the US National Center for Health Statistics that asked specific questions about stress levels, stress management, and perceptions about how stress affects health. They used a sample of about 29,000 respondents from the survey who matched up to public records and looked at instances of death among survey respondents through 2006. Overall, they found that survey respondents who reported a lot of stress and held a perception that stress had a significant impact on health had an increased hazard ratio that converted to a 43% increased risk of premature death. However, survey respondents who reported a lot of stress but little or no perception that stress impacted health had the lowest hazard ratio of any group in the survey, even among those who felt almost no stress.

Now that is interesting.

So, what you believe about stress can have a major impact on what stress can do to you. Unfortunately, as the data could only be collected retrospectively, that is, by looking at mortality figures from the National Death Index, it's somewhat difficult to discover where those beliefs came from. Either way, the conclusion of the study states, "High amounts of stress and the perception that stress impacts health is each associated with poor physical and mental health. Individuals who perceived that stress affected their health and reported a large amount of stress had an increased risk of premature death".

There are other positive insights to stress, too, although mostly conducted in animal studies. They include finding that stress may help you connect with your instincts and in the short term, at least, can help improve performance. In this study, students were asked to complete a very stressful and complicated task followed by a simpler and easier to do task. It was discovered that the more stressed they were in the first task, the better they performed later. You may find this, too, that having been stressed for a short burst, you are more likely to tap into your instincts when facing a less stressful task very soon afterwards.

This is much like driving on a motorway, then turning off and having to drive more slowly into a town. Neurologically we are still set up to be driving at speed and can make much quicker decisions, despite the reduction in our driving speed.

Animal studies have also shown how stress can help you improve your memory and, in another study, help improve learning. How all this relates to humans is still under investigation, but any parent of a teenager about to take an important exam might wonder if there is any truth at all in these studies.

However, I am more interested in the study from Wisconsin-Madison as to how we form beliefs and, in particular, how we form the belief that stress is harmful. The foundations of our beliefs, as we know them, are almost all formed in us, or programmed into us, at a very early age, typically up to seven years old. Yes, that's right, pretty much everything we know to be true and how we make sense of what's going on around us has its foundations in our early childhood, at a time when our brains are still maturing and when we have little capacity to form argument or reasoning. Basically, all we are doing in this early stage of growth is figuring out how we survive in the system we have been born into. Our reptilian brain, the amygdala, is the only part of our brain that is mature, and it acts as a radar, constantly scanning our environment and checking for danger. Oddly, we can survive in some terrible conditions, and learning what is survivable programs us for the future. So, if we are fortunate to have been loved in our upbringing, we will know how to love as an adult. If love is denied to us as a child, love from our parents, guardians, or whatever system we were born into, we will grow up believing we are unlovable. If an infant craves love and it is denied, the infant believes it to be their fault and takes ownership of that belief, sometimes into lonely adulthood.

So, knowing this, holding the belief that stress is bad for you must come from a learned behaviour or observation early in our lives, and it's quite easy to see how this could happen. A child as young as 14 months old can understand the gender roles of their parents (assuming a male-female partnership). In same-sex partnerships, they will still know who is who and which buttons to push to get what they want. People also sometimes recognise that the first negative emotion in their lives comes from an event before they were born. The foetus can pick up on emotions and bring awareness with them when they are born. They can't make any sense of this knowledge at the time but can recognise its effect on them as adults.

These early formed beliefs, often known as core beliefs, are formed unconsciously in these early years. They are also strongly connected to our values which are those things we are willing to expend resources for or to obtain resources to have. Largely unconscious, values drive a person's true purpose as a human being. Values govern all human behaviour and are the way we decide good and bad, right and wrong, and appropriate or not. The highly valued criteria are the big ones, the ones around which we form our beliefs.

Our core beliefs and values are the most pervasive. These impact us the most and are, unfortunately, mostly outside our awareness. They are what define our personality and, ultimately, our behaviour, given that behaviour is an external manifestation of our emotions and thoughts. The good news is that as we have been taught, in some capacity, almost everything we think we know, we can also be un-taught, if that's a thing, or rather reprogrammed. The only fears we are born with are the fear of loud noises and of falling. Everything else is a learned behaviour. The more we believe something, of course, we see evidence to confirm the belief until it becomes fact. So, if we believe stress is bad for us and will kill us if left unchecked, we will see lots of evidence, usually from others, that this is true, and so it goes.

I encountered a perfect example of this while I was running a workshop for leaders in a global organisation. I tell you this as if it could happen here, it could happen anywhere. The group was asked to complete a task between the end of the current module and the beginning of the next in about six weeks' time. It was a simple enough task in that all they had to do was reach out to as yet unmet people in their place of work to increase the size of their current network by just ten people. Now, I imagine for some people, just two would be stressful enough, but, given the size of the organisation, ten was a very easy target.

After a couple of minutes of thinking about who they might like to add to their list, one lady said:

"Oh... I've tried this, and it doesn't work".

"Oh, that's interesting", I said, "Perhaps you need to find a different approach, a different way to get what you want".

"Yes, I've tried that as well", she said, "and that doesn't work either!"

"Aha", I said, "Now that sounds as though you have developed a self-limiting belief".

"What do you mean?" she asked.

"Well, you tried to do something once, and it didn't work, so you tried again, and it didn't work again, so now you believe that whatever you do, it won't work, to the point that it doesn't work and you just give yourself more evidence to support your self-limiting belief that it won't work... and so it doesn't," I suggested.

She sat back, thoughtfully contemplating what had just passed. There was also a noticeable shift in energy in the room as people got a little agitated when someone on the other side of the room spoke out, "But surely that's a fact!" he stated.

Oooh... the room bristled with anticipation as I had been challenged.

I agreed; it was a fact. The room relaxed, until I followed up with, based on her belief.

The 12 heads in the room "exploded" with this thought.

It was a good explosion, though, as several of this group sought me out afterwards and said that this exchange was news to them, and suddenly, in that moment, they had seen some of the beliefs they held about themselves and how they had been holding them back. Even better was that the lady with the original self-limiting belief went away and pushed through it, and so expanded her network.

Is it time for you to update your internal operating system too? My wife and I can also experience the same event differently, notably a ride on a roller coaster. Fairly close to where we live is one of Europe's best amusement parks which boasts the tallest ride in Europe, the *Silver Star*. By almost all roller coaster criteria, this one is quite tame as there are no loops in it at all, just ups and downs... at speed.

We've been on this ride together just once.

It was more than enough for my wife as we reached its peak of 73 metres, just to get started, to get up to the maximum speed of 103 km/hr and pulling 4G. Like all these rides, if you pick your times badly, you end up queuing for far longer than the three minutes spent on the ride, but despite sitting next to each other and experiencing the same conditions at the same time, we had different experiences. For my wife, it was terror. Her amygdala had spiked, and there was cortisol coursing through her veins, and with no means of escape, this was going to be doing some vascular damage. The whole ride was a terrifying and fearful experience… for her. For me, however, the exact opposite was true. I loved every climb of anticipation, and the release of the downward slopes thrilled me, so the amount of cortisol in my system dropped as it was replaced by DHEA, the so-called youth hormone.

The fun I experienced, which turned into joy and laughter, had become a positive growth experience with a different set of hormones rushing through my body.

Same experience, different outcome, and a choice you can make to make the difference.

You and Your Stressors: How to Overcome Your Stuck Points

Stress can creep up on you in many ways, from physical and behavioural symptoms that are obvious to subtler symptoms that mess with your emotional and cognitive state of being. Yet, each time, it can leave behind a somewhat similar and familiar feeling, the feeling of being a little more lost, battered, and alone.

No stressed person has the same set of symptoms, which is why each person's experience is unique and, therefore, their individual journey. That said, most people have some of each type of the symptom, only in different combinations, which makes understanding how it works more appreciable. The remainder of this chapter focuses on personality concepts that will help you understand how your stress and anxiety work.

The Multifaceted You

Now, you cannot look at the average stressed-out person to understand your situation. You don't need to. You need to understand the many dimensions within you in which your anxiety and stress exist. Once you start identifying these dimensions, which are mostly characterised by triggers and symptoms, you'll be able to work around them and in time, overcome them too.

Some things you may now like to do …

Exercise 1 - What Do You See?

Here's a quick worksheet for you. Do any of these situations sound familiar to you?

- You dislike change; every time you are put into a new situation, you feel restless and worried.
- You over process information, decisions, and possibilities before acting.
- You tend to be pessimistic about the present and future.
- You constantly dwell on negative past experiences.
- You worry about everything.
- You feel awkward when someone compliments you; you also believe they don't mean their compliments or are mocking you in some way.

You are, after all, your harshest critic.

While there is no scoring system here to rate your anxiety, it does help you to understand whether you are anxiety-prone. The more items you tick, the more likely you are suffering from anxiety, depression, or both.

Understanding Your Anxiety and What It Is Doing to You

Anxiety on the inside can affect how you act on the outside. And so, if you were to observe your mind and body carefully, you might be able to notice some signs, both behavioural and physical, that could tell you what your anxiety might be doing to you. For instance, an anxious person might be dealing with several conflicting and apprehensive thoughts. The internal noise and fear that reverberates might make them appear tired, withdrawn, and/ or nervous.

Exercise 2 - What Does Your Behaviour Say about You?

Tick the statements that apply to you:

- I find myself crying for no reason.
- There are times when I feel empty and can't make myself do what I want to do.
- I avoid socialising.
- I avoid risks.
- I avoid doing fun stuff because I worry about the possible risk involved.
- I'm afraid of failure and judgement.
- I get fidgety.
- I obsess over the past, worry about the future, and can rarely stay in the present.

And About Your Body?

- I have no appetite.
- I'm always hungry.
- My palms sweat all the time.
- I can feel nauseous, lightheaded, cold, and shaky when anxious.
- My heart races when I worry.
- I feel cold and weak.

Again, there is no scoring system to rate you. The more symptoms you tick, the more likely you are stressed and experiencing anxiety. Note: Some of the above symptoms can also result from various other reasons, so we suggest you consult your primary care physician before making any conclusions.

Reflecting upon Your Triggers and Identifying Beliefs That are Standing in Your Way

If you could follow an anxious mind, you might see patterns of unfavourable thoughts that play on and off. These thoughts might be triggers to the anxiety itself, so addressing them is very important. A clinical technique called imagery exposure, used in therapy can help address the triggers as well as identify their sources.

Exercise 3 - Imagery Exposure

Sit with yourself and truthfully reflect on any unfavourable thoughts that play in your mind; the thoughts that stop you from concentrating and being in the present, the ones that you want to forget but cannot, and the ones that you might have kept buried and might not necessarily like to share with others. You can also reflect on any worry thoughts, the ones that haven't happened yet but that you fear.

Recall the sights and sounds of the situation as if it were happening in front of you, as we speak, in as much detail as you can. Bring the image of the embarrassment, avoidance, worry, fear, hurt, and/ or guilt vividly to mind. Deliberate on the image, living the experience thoroughly once.

Let the thoughts stay with you until they decide to leave you at their will. Repeat this exercise once every day for as long as you want. As you progress further, you'll begin to see reasons. You'll recognise beliefs that have been blocking your path, your stuck points, so to speak. You'll find solutions to overcome the negative outcomes of your triggers. Finally, you'll find peace.

This Is Just the Start

Now, this is a gradual process and is the first step to addressing your anxiety. Once you know what's causing your anxiety, you can, in time, find ways to manage or overcome it, and this book shows you exactly how to do that.

Mindfully Moving Beyond the Beliefs Blocking Your Path

The thing about stuck points is that when we're caught in one, we don't often think about ways to work around them and move forward. We don't shift into problem-solving mode and weigh our options, mostly because we don't know how to and, therefore, cannot.

To be able to solve problems, you must think realistically, coherently, and without any chatter. Unfortunately, when anxious, our mind can get tied up in its contemplation wheel and fail to work on more productive and purposeful things.

For instance, imagine you have a team deadline to meet, but a member of your team isn't contributing equally. Instead of working yourself up about why they aren't doing their bit, it would be more useful to think about ways to help them step up or help reach the immediate deadline.

So, you can:

- Speak to the member and let them know where they need to step up while suggesting some options to work things out.
- Give them simpler jobs or a checklist to do every day.
- Split the work amongst others in the team.
- Get the job done first and then look at a more permanent way out.

Mindfully forcing yourself to look at the possible solutions as opposed to mulling on the problem can help relieve the stress of rumination. Focusing on a constructive solution will shift you to a more positive state of mind, just as achieving the solution will shift you to a state of peace and contentment.

Exercise 4 - Recognising Your Challenges

- Reflect on the one stuck point that is stopping you from moving forward.
- Define your best three realistic solutions: keep them simple and achievable.
- Decide what you need to do to act on them.
- Decide how long you need to gather these tools.
- Start working towards these goals.

Where to Next?

At this point, you should pat yourself on the back. You've made progress and are a step closer to understanding and managing your anxiety. The next few chapters discuss aspects that go a little beyond your thoughts. They dwell on areas like your mind and body and their role in your anxiety. Take a moment to pause now and then.

Stay in the present.

This is your reality.

Where do you want to be?

Ok, let's start preparing for your future.

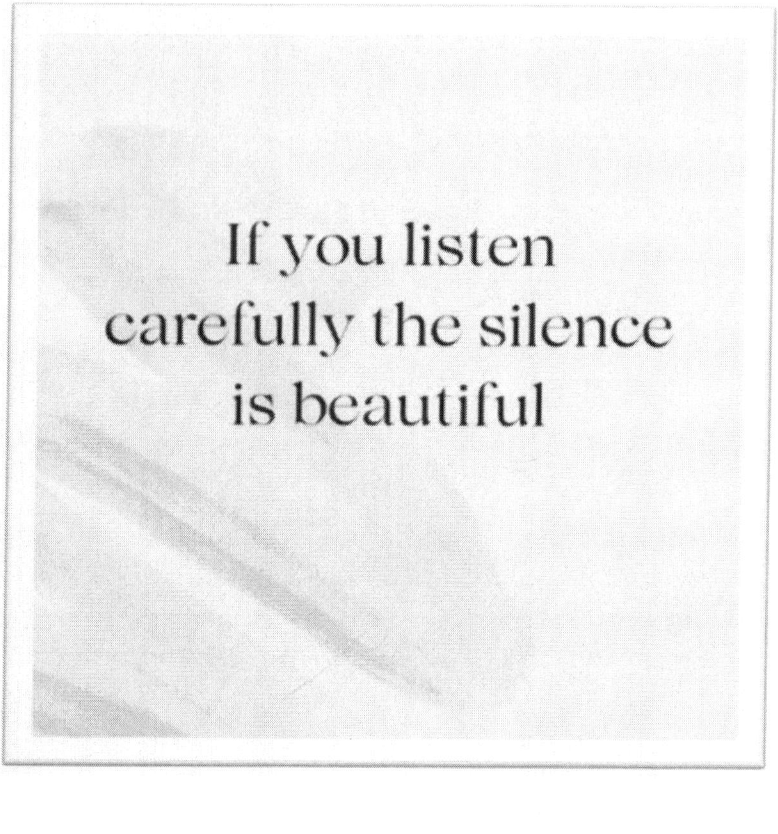
If you listen
carefully the silence
is beautiful

CHAPTER 4

Your Powerful Mindset

As creatures of habit, we like nothing more than to be with the familiar. We have the innate capacity to be able to learn from now and hold that learning, so when something the same or even remotely similar comes along, we just dig into our memory bank, look at the relevant "how-to" files, and do the task. It's a good system, without which we would all need to re-learn how to write our name, button our shirt, or sing Happy Birthday every time we wanted to.

The challenge with such habitual behaviour is that we switch off from being in the moment and being totally present. I'll touch on this a bit more in the chapter on Emotional Intelligence, but for now, it's interesting to know that there isn't a single decision we take on an hour-by-hour basis that doesn't first rush through the emotional centres of our brain, and yet we don't notice it anymore.

Also, today our capacity to do more and more and take increasingly demanding decisions is on the increase, which is why slowing down and clearing some of that noise will support our powerful mindset. It begins with where and how we place our awareness, how consistently we evaluate what we are doing, and our ability to understand and build resilience.

I think it's fair to say that many of us face pretty much the same fears and challenges that test our mindset. Just thinking about this for a moment and being aware of it now will help us overcome all challenges we face in our way consistently and help build our powerful mindset.

There's a quote that comes from the great and widely respected philosopher, Captain Jack Sparrow from the Pirates of the Caribbean franchise, where, faced with a seemingly insurmountable problem, he says, "It's not the problem that's the problem, it's your attitude to the problem that's the problem". And I think he's right. In essence, it's your mindset. Generate a powerful resource and flexible mindset, and there is nowhere for stress to live. It will go away. In terms of mindset, it turns out we can be categorised into three broad groups. They are victim, survivor, and thriver, each having their own special characteristics.

The *victims* are those people who think the world happens "to them". Maybe you know someone who thinks that the world owes them a job or, through no effort on their part, they deserve a pay rise or promotion. These people also fail to take responsibility for where they are now in their life, instead blaming their situation and circumstance on the government or the economy, or, in fact, almost anyone other than their own choices, however ill-informed those choices may have been. No, it's definitely not their fault. Life happens to these people, and they respond rather than taking control and going for it and getting what they want out of life.

Survivors take a different point of view and have different mindsets. These people have fought through a very difficult time and feel they must continue to fight. Success can only come from hard work that delivers its own rewards, and yet, despite all their efforts, which could well bring some success, they never give up. Everything is a challenge and a challenge worth fighting for. However, success is never easy.

The *thrivers,* by contrast, are insatiably curious and want to thrive. They see that they have choices and are openly curious as to which one they should be taking. The funny thing is, they never make a bad decision because if the decision they took doesn't quite get them what they were after, they adjust things. Being flexible and curious in the moment enables them to get what they are after. The thriver epitomises the notion that the only bad decision is the one not taken, as that just delays progress.

The challenge we all have is that we can jump around these three mindsets depending on our circumstances. The trick is to be open to this and become aware when we do. Through this self-reflection, we can train ourselves and develop our mindset into a powerful one. Here are some things you can do now to start moving in the right direction:

Define your needs:

1. Biological and physiological needs.
1. Safety needs.
1. Belongingness and love needs.
1. Esteem needs.
1. Self-actualisation needs.

This will help you understand where both you and your clients are coming from.

Self-care

- Fill your cup first; you can't help others if you don't have your cup filled
- Your happy place: what does that mean to you? What makes YOU happy?
- This will be your pillar of strength.

Emotional resilience

- Building up your resilience will help you manage stress better and overcome your fear, sense of failure, and adversity.
- Stress stems from our emotions. Once we know this, we can really elevate humanity.
- Setbacks are going to show up, but having a strong mindset will help you move forward.

Be patient with yourself. Master what you're building, one step at a time. Don't compare yourself with anybody else because we are all on different journeys.

Focus your energy on showing up consistently and doing what you must do.

I use an approach called CAVAC as a starting point:

C: Compassion
A: being Authentic
V: being Vulnerable
A: Adaptability
C: Courage and Curiosity

Many people look to outside factors and their surroundings to find inner peace without even realising it. Inner peace can only come from within and stems from our deeply rooted beliefs about ourselves and the way we react to different situations.

You have likely experienced many beliefs subconsciously that sink your sense of self-confidence and overall happiness. By analysing the thoughts and beliefs that occur in your mind each day, you can shift to a more positive and confident outlook on life, full of peace and serenity.

"Once I get what I want, I will feel better".

This belief is a very common way that we get wrapped up in our surroundings and allow them to guide us and determine our well-being. When we understand that feeling good and being happy come from within, we will no longer experience these restricting views.

To truly practise gratitude and be present in the moment, we must allow our inner peace to guide us, regardless of our situations or aspirations. Although it is important to have desires and goals, it is vital not to let them determine our quality of life and inner satisfaction.

"People are always out to get me".

Although we do not usually say this out loud, our subconscious holds restricting beliefs like these that prevent us from achieving our goals and aspirations. When you are constantly focused on what others think of you and how they will react, the anxiety guides your life, and you will not feel at peace on the inside.

Rather than expecting people to go against you, accept the fact that not everyone will like you and let go of seeking approval from others. Allowing others to have their opinions and not being afraid of them or letting them get in the way of your views can release you to get a lot further in your life than you would expect.

"I should be able to work harder".

Comparing our work ethic or other components of our

lives, like appearance or social skills, blocks our confidence and prevents us from experiencing inner peace. Although you may look at others and think they are better than you, you must realise that everyone is different, and comparison can only hold you back.

Focusing on how you can improve your qualities and traits rather than trying to be like someone else can make you feel less stressed, and you will, in turn, have higher confidence levels.

Comparison can have negative impacts on friendships and even relationships and will always get in the way of inner joy and happiness.

"I could never do that".

Doubting yourself and your capabilities is one of the most powerful ways that your subconscious restricts you from achieving your desires and goals. When you see someone performing on stage or completing something you have always aspired to do, it can be easy to think that you could never be capable of it.

When you think like this, you can't have the confidence you need to accomplish these things. Taking a step back and realising that you can accomplish anything that you put your mind to will allow you to be more motivated and at peace from within.

"Inner peace is impossible".

When we read books about meditation and other peace techniques, it can be easy to feel overwhelmed and not capable. It can feel like these qualities take years and years to build up, and we must make a lot of sacrifices to experience inner peace.

Often, the best way to find inner peace is by letting go of these assumptions and just starting with slowly adjusting your daily life. You will likely see results sooner than you think, and inner peace will naturally flow.

If you're reading this book, you probably experience stress and anxiety in some form or another but don't know where those feelings come from. This is completely normal and a sign that you are ready - ready to understand the origins of your emotions and ready to work your way around and overcome them. This chapter shows you how to address your mental and physical battles while digging deeper into the source of your anxiety, your inner demons, so to speak.

The confusion and anxiety you feel today could be the result of seeds planted in your past. So, delving into your past, into memories that you perhaps would otherwise like to avoid and forget or have consciously erased from your mind, can help piece together the source of your anxiety.

Disclaimer: Some memories you revisit through the questions put forth in this chapter may bring up unexpected reactions, and that's completely normal. It's OK. You may feel slightly uncomfortable, and that's normal too. As unexpected and unpleasant as they can be, these reactions are significant as they may lead you to the origins of your problems. That said, if you become overtly overwhelmed, I recommend you stop the exercise and seek professional help. I do recommend you also have someone who can have your back to be nearby for support.

Exercise 5 - Review Your World

People who are stressed and anxious often know they are experiencing those feelings. They can tell you how they feel but don't know why they feel that way. That's why journaling can be such a significant tool to help address and overcome this emotional state.

Here are some suggestions for you to do right now:

Daily, for two weeks at least, mindfully observe your thoughts, emotions, and bodily reactions. This will increase your self-awareness.

Ask yourself what is going on when you start noticing your emotions and body signals. Write your experiences when they are fresh. Remember, all emotions are information. All I'm asking here is for you to decide what that information means for you. Use feeling words to describe any powerful and/ or repetitive emotion. For instance, happy, energetic, nervous, sweaty, tired, dizzy, and so on.

Because we want to know the cause of your emotions, especially note down the feelings that make you feel anxious or stressed. Make a note of the situations that led up to this state.

At the end of the second week, or more often if you wish, reflect on your feelings and situations. Compare them with your notes from exercise 4 (previous chapter).

Do you see a pattern? Make a note of your thoughts.

Imagining the Worst

Life can be rough sometimes. Bad things can happen without a plan and can leave behind a sense of lasting pain and fear. But sometimes, our minds can fantasise about things that never happened and probably never will. These things can be our biggest fears. We can imagine catastrophic events and jump to the worst possible conclusions with no reason or logic, and by doing so repeatedly, we live the experience that many times. The reason is that your mind and body might not be able to differentiate the real from the imaginary world.

Self-Blame. Self-Loathing. All of it.

Rachel suffers from constant worry and anxiety. She says some of this is the result of the busy life she leads. She wakes up at 5 a.m. every day, travels an hour to reach work, is constantly rushing through meetings and deadlines, takes another hour to reach home at 8 p.m., cooks and finishes her dinner, and prepares for the next day before she can go to sleep at 11 p.m.

Sometimes things get rough, and her anxiety kicks in based on her worst imagination. Here's how she says her mind plays out events when that happens, resulting in her blaming and hating herself.

'My throat hurts. I think I can feel a lump. What if it's cancer? Am I going to die? What will happen to my family once I'm gone? Will they miss me?

I remember a bad/ traumatic experience and replay that event repeatedly, imagining it is happening again. Sometimes I imagine it being worse, and my responses are very real.

I see a group of people giggling in front of me. Are they laughing at me? Is it my dress? Do I look OK? Did I do something odd or funny? I need to get out of here. Why do people always make fun of me? I don't deserve this. Nobody likes me. I'm hopeless.

My manager didn't greet me as usual. I wonder if they are upset about my work. What if I get fired? What about my bills? Why can't I do anything right? Why am I never good enough? I hate myself.

Exercise 6 - Living Your Biggest Fears

This time, with reason, decide to live your biggest fears once again, but this time more mindfully. Take one fear at a time, and if there are many, move over to the next fear only after you've completely made peace with the current one. Sure, this might take time, but the positive effects can last a lifetime. So, don't rush. Again, decide whether you want to have someone around to watch your back.

Sit with yourself when you're feeling most secure and comfortable. Remind yourself that what you are going to experience isn't real. Remind yourself to disconnect from the emotional trauma you are knowingly going to put yourself through. Remind yourself of the purpose of this exercise. You want to dig deeper into your fears and understand what you are learning from them. Once you recognise this, you can work on the learning, and the suffering will gradually decrease.

When you're ready, go through the experience of your biggest fears, the worst possible situations, your inner demons, so to speak. What keeps troubling you? Why do you keep inviting this experience into your life? Is there a lesson to be learned?

What's the worst possible that can happen? OK, that happened. Can it get worse? Imagine that too. Live the experience, all the time telling yourself that this isn't real and isn't happening now.

Again, when you're ready, bring yourself back to the present and reflect on your thoughts and emotions. Write them down when you are ready.

Repeat this exercise whenever you are ready and until you've made peace with the fear and can move on.

The best way to gain perspective is to mindfully talk to yourself as you experience the rush of fantasised images. Now that you know that that can happen, the next time you catch yourself doing something like that, tell yourself:

- This isn't real, and it's not happening now.
- Whatever happens, I can cope.
- I am going to stop causing my suffering.
- I am doing great; I've got this.
- I love myself; I feel great.

Connecting Them with Your Mind and Body

Remember, you can manage and even overcome your anxiety by learning to feel better with introspection. Ask yourself as many questions about your anxiety as you can. Persist because, deep down, you have and know the answers. Observe your relationship with your feelings and thoughts and your body's responses to them. Track them and talk yourself to a better, calmer, and more panic-free state of mind. Yes, you can!

Exercise 7 - Talking Yourself Out of Anxiety

- Each day, record events that make you anxious. Elaborate and specify the event as well as your thoughts and bodily reactions to it.
- Use feeling words to describe your emotions.
- Go through the experience and decide to make peace with it.
- Keep telling yourself that the present is great, and the future will be even better.
- Work on your feelings. Talk to yourself. Gather support from others if you want to.
- At the end of every week, look back on your tracker and evaluate your progress.
- How are you feeling?

As you work through the exercises presented in this book, you should become more aware of your anxiety and the reasons for it as well as how your body reacts to events in your life. The more knowledge you gain, the better you can understand and manage your anxiety.

So, keep at it.

The problem is not the problem. The problem is your attitude about the problem.

Captain Jack Sparrow

CHAPTER 5

... and Breathe

In the previous chapter, we looked at improving your mindset to show up as the best you in the best possible state, that state where you know you're in control and your head is clear. What a lot of people do not yet realise is that it's your breathing pattern and the thoughts that go along with how you are breathing that can have a direct impact on your ability to have that powerful mindset. It's true!

Let's go back to the beginning. After our safe arrival on this planet, most of us were in a fairly relaxed and safe environment. The only mature part of our brain at this stage of life is the reptilian brain, controlling our vital functions such as heart rate, breathing, body temperature, and balance. It's very reliable but tends to be somewhat rigid and compulsive. Most importantly, though, this part of our brain is on constant alert for our well-being, scanning non-stop, like a radar, to figure out if we are safe or in danger.

Because it's only concerned with our survival and, with that, the reproductive success of our genes, it will guide us to always be careful with our choices in any situation – to move away from something that might put us in harm's way and head towards a place of safety. This part of the brain is working at the subconscious level and using learned behaviour as we pick our way through our environment. The reptilian brain helps us develop patterns of behaviour for survival, even if those patterns are surviving in a bad place. Survival is the key.

Now, let's assume that we are essentially in a safe environment, and we are not being threatened minute by minute. In most parts of the world, we have evolved into a much calmer way of living compared with our Neanderthal ancestors. As we move around our towns and cities, we are not threatened in the same way they were.

But back to the newly born infant.

Anyone who has ever seen a small child will know that when they lay on their backs and breathe, they are breathing through their diaphragm into their belly. The rhythm of their breathing is even, with each in and out breath lasting for about the same time. They are relaxed. Somehow, in the modern world, we have lost this ability to tap into our breathing in this relaxed, steady way and so find it hard to be in that relaxed state again. However, all is not lost, and we can re-learn it.

It might be interesting to find out why we don't breathe in the way that supports us best and why we should benefit from re-learning how to breathe "properly". I mean, breathing is just natural, isn't it? It's something we just do, so why on earth would you want to examine how you breathe and find out if there's a better way to do it, to help clear your head to get ahead?

It is true we were never taught to breathe; we just did it. It really is one of the most natural things we do, and as children, we did breathe in the most supportive rhythmic way. But then we went to school! Things change at school, and one of the things most schools introduce is some sort of physical exercise, then later competitive sports. When playing a sport, we move from being in that relaxed state with easy rhythmic breathing into one of high energy and high oxygen demand when our breathing pattern has to change. We now start to learn a new way of breathing and move away from our belly breathing into our chests. When I first learned about this, I guess my response might have been like yours - I asked why we don't just revert to belly breathing when the exercise is over? It's a good question, and no one has figured out an answer yet.

Breathing is not only crucial for survival but also for relaxing. Many of my clients also like to take care of their physical well-being, which is great, and many of them do so with aerobic activity. One of the easiest and least expensive ways to maintain a level of fitness is by running, and it is exactly this sort of client with a high-powered corporate job who runs for relaxation that has difficulty with belly breathing. Running for fitness is good, don't get me wrong, but it trains the subconscious to learn a different way of breathing and to use different muscle groups for breathing. As with any aerobic activity, we need to fuel our muscles with oxygen and take out the carbon dioxide, the exhaust fumes if you like. The higher the level of exercise, the faster this oxygen exchange needs to happen, and the only way our system can keep up is with rapid breathing. At the same time, our vagus nerve, the wandering nerve, kicks into action and stimulates our heart muscles with adrenaline which keeps the system pumping. This is exactly what happens when I ask clients to "take a deep breath". Their chest expands, filling the upper part of their body and... stimulating their vagus nerve, which releases adrenaline and, well... you get the picture.

Diaphragmatic or belly breathing happens a lot lower down, and the expansion happens through the belly and not up in the chest. Remember the baby from earlier? Imagine it lying on its back and just breathing. Its little belly is just going up and down, and that's what we need to get back to help our breathing keep us in a relaxed state. If you are about to walk out on stage to deliver your keynote speech, make sure that your instruction to "take a deep breath" is actioned down through your belly; it'll make all the difference.

However, it seems there is more to this breathing thing than we might first have imagined. By now, you get the idea that exercise requires us to take short gasping breaths to satisfy our oxygen needs. In fact, if you want to pump yourself up, you can get your heart racing by just panting. In a very short time, your heart rate will increase without you actually exercising. It turns out that the opposite is also true. Taking long breaths in and out has a calming effect on your system. To calm yourself down, and it only takes two or three breaths to do this, just breathe in for less time than you breathe out. Figures like 7 / 11 or 5 / 8 are often quoted as the counts you make to yourself and in your head for the length of in and out breaths, respectively. Now, 7 / 11 doesn't mean seven seconds in and 11 seconds out; it's just a count that suits you at the time you do this. If 7 / 11 is too long, try 5 / 8 or something in between that you can do with a consistent shorter in-breath and a longer out-breath.

Exercise 8: Give it a go

As you are breathing, place your right hand on your chest with your right little finger either on or as close as you can get to the bottom of your rib cage, and sit your left hand gently on your belly. As you breathe in and out, your right hand shouldn't move, while your left hand should gently move in and out as you breathe into your belly. I know it's not a sexy look, but it is something that will help you in the moment. As you practise this with a group of like-minded friends or in private, you will start to learn which muscle groups to use so that, in time, you will be able to breathe through your belly without the help of placing your hands on your chest and belly. When you can do that, no one will know what you are doing, although they will want to know how you can sit there in that high-pressure meeting and remain calm and, more significantly, focused.

Before we move on from breathing, there's more. The belly breathing technique will be able to relax you in the moment or keep you super relaxed. It helps fill your brain with oxygen and physiologically cannot fail to calm you. With practice, you will be able to use it automatically. But there's more.

Belly breathing isn't always appropriate and could be seen as a rescue after a moment of overwhelm or stressful outburst. Maybe something more appropriate for the modern workplace is balanced breathing. In balanced breathing, the in- and out-breaths are the same length. On a normal day, with moments of stress and confusion, our heart rate fluctuates. This fluctuation, a little like driving a car in bursts of speed then stopping, isn't that good for heart health, and a more sustainable, even rhythm is preferred. After all, you get much better fuel economy when driving on a long motorway journey compared with driving around town. This time, instead of 7 / 11 breathing, our count is five or six for both the in and out breaths. Do this for just five minutes, three times a day or just a minute or two each hour, and you will soon discover the world of relaxed alertness, that amazing state of being relaxed enough to be in the best state possible to do what needs to be done yet alert enough to act when needed.

The next and final stage in breathing to clear your head is to change your focus as you do it. Your focus needs to be on your breathing, and the best way I have discovered to do this is just to focus on the very tip of your nose and sense the change in temperature as you breathe in. The in-breath is cooler than the out-breath. According to the HeartMath® Institute, even more benefits can be found by imagining your breathing going in and out of your heart by focusing on your heart as you breathe. When you have got the hang of this and while still breathing in this steady rhythm, recall a time when you felt great or when you cared for someone in your life. Holding a memory, such as care or appreciation, with this positive emotion attached to it will start to remove the stress from your system and quickly. Stepping into a genuine state of gratitude is even better. If you find this tricky, just ask yourself, what are you thankful for?

Here's a thought. At those moments in life when you've attained success, it's so easy to be grateful right there in that moment, but have you considered gratitude in advance? Think about it this way: When we express gratitude, we're seeing the good in a situation. Gratitude in the moment will have you looking for the good right now, where you are.

So, stop what you're doing. What can you be grateful for right now? Perhaps the obstacle you're facing is pointing you in a new direction; failure means you've discovered a way something hasn't worked before. Or, if you're slogging through what feels like many tedious steps, you can, instead, be grateful that you're moving forward and making progress on your journey.

This, my friend, is focusing on the moment and finding the good right now.

The science behind this is fascinating, and I recommend you read **Transforming Stress** by Doc Childre and Deborah

Rozman for a fuller explanation. Essentially, the heart is the centre of your energy, and by focusing on your heart as you breathe with a steady rhythm, and step back into or hold that memory, the heart rate steadies, which, in turn, affects the brain and relieves stress in the moment. It's a technique known as Quick Coherence®.

Nothing worth having is easy, although mastering the Quick Coherence® technique is not that difficult and certainly easier than learning German as a second language. It will take a little time and daily practice to truly master, but as the results and changes happen quickly, I am sure you will find the benefits outweigh the effort taken to get there.

Relaxation takes effort and needs to be practised.

Breathing, or taking a breath, can bring a dramatic change in the outcome of a stressful confrontation, as we'll see in the next chapter.

Some more things to do now.

Practising Stillness

When you hear the word "stillness", you probably think of the act of physically sitting still without any sounds, movements, or feelings. This is true, in a sense, but stillness also refers to a sense of inner peace and serenity (or calmness). Because stillness involves the body, mind, and spirit, you can practise stillness in many ways and improve your overall mental state. Let's go over some of the easiest ways that you can practise stillness in your life right now!

1. Take Time to Reflect

How often do you find yourself just going through the motions of life and never looking back? While this is a good strategy to avoid harping on negatives and reliving bad experiences, it also denies you the opportunity to reflect. One of the best ways to practise stillness is by sitting down and reflecting on past events that you have experienced. Think about things that have happened, ideally happy moments, and think about what they meant to you and how they've changed you for the better as a person.

2. Focus on Gratitude and What You're Thankful For

As humans, we spend a lot of time looking toward the future and constantly setting new goals. This is great for advancing yourself as a functioning member of society, but it's also good to slow down a little and look around. Take time to think about what you currently have in your life. This could be friends, family, physical items, and experiences you've had. Just focus on the positives that have happened in your life, identify what you're thankful for, and jot them down in a gratitude journal.

3. Just "Be"

How often do you just merely "exist" as a human? We're talking about just sitting or lying, not doing anything productive, not thinking about anything that's going on in your life, and not being distracted by your phone or other technology. Take the time to just relax and do nothing. You can do it in your home or at your favourite place; just focus on breathing, passing by any negative thoughts that might be lingering, and work on the concept of existing.

4. Try Meditation

It's hard to go a minute in your life without being stressed by something, let alone being stress-free for an hour or more.

Therefore, it's a great idea to proactively rid your mind of the stress you're experiencing, at least for a little while.

Find a comfortable spot and play some soft music or a guided meditation track. Focus on taking deep breaths, clearing your mind of any lingering stress, and shifting your mind toward nothing (yes, nothing at all!).

5. Explore the World

When was the last time you went more than 30 minutes away from your house (not including work or the supermarket)? Now, think about the last time you went off the beaten path and explored nature. You don't have to go on a road trip or go anywhere further than the local hiking trails at the park, but spend a little time engulfing yourself in the beauty of the world around you, and you'll begin to recognise that there's much more to life than your little world.

When you begin to actively practise stillness in your life, you'll notice that you feel much calmer than normal. It takes a bit of time and effort on your part, but this is honestly one of the best ways to achieve a sense of inner peace. Once we have started to develop this quieter space, it's possible to develop our ability to focus and maintain that focus. Focusing comes in different forms for everyone; some like listening to music, while others want complete silence. Below are some suggestions that can help you find your focus.

Evidence shows that waking up every morning with a plan of what your day will look like is beneficial. This doesn't have to be a detailed schedule that outlines every minute, but having a plan will eliminate small decisions that can take you off track. Having a plan will also give you a clear goal for how your day should progress and end. Take time every evening to write out, not just in your head, the plan for the next day. It can include what you will have for breakfast through to what order you will complete your work in. It may also be helpful to prep items such as meals, coffee, and clothing to keep you on track. The first thing is also one of the best times to meditate or practise the heart-focused breathing described earlier. Somehow, giving even a short amount of time to the practice at the end of the day saves time later.

Every day, take at least a small amount of time to do something you really enjoy. This can be peace and quiet over your morning coffee, a short walk in the afternoon, or snuggles with a pet or loved one in the evening. Having that moment of enjoyment will give you a respite from all the to-dos that fill your day and will allow time to reset and prepare for what comes next.

If a task isn't coming easily to you, feel free to walk away for a few minutes or even a day. However, don't give up on it; instead, be persistent with the process. Allowing yourself to bounce from task to task to avoid difficult work will leave you with a list of half-done tasks and a brain running in a million different directions. Better yet, make sure you do your least enjoyable tasks first thing in your working day, so the rest of the day has more joy in it.

"There's no rest for the wicked, and the righteous don't need it" is a familiar turn of phrase that praises busy people. But we all know that it isn't true. Take time off if you can. We all need a day off to rest, reset, and recuperate. We also need time with our families and friends to fill our cups and remind us that the hard days are worth it. If full days are tricky, then moments during the day can be used to just clear your head and slow down. Even if it's just five minutes, it will soon pay dividends.

Focusing better is both a mindset and physical act that you must prepare your mind and body for. Be sure you are doing everything in your power to set yourself up to the best of your ability.

Under the obsessive
thoughts and plans,
under the emotions,
positive and negative,
there is an ocean of
peace.

Gangaji

CHAPTER 6

Let It Go

Depending on the nature of the beast you are working with, the very idea of "letting it go" can be easy to say and tricky to do. However, by hanging on to that thing you can't let go of, maybe an argument or a difference of opinion, and figuring out who is right just feeds the negative energy associated with it. The moment has gone; it's over, finished with, so let it go.

I'm constantly reminded of this as my clients come in with all sorts of unfairness, for example, at work, that absorbs a huge amount of brainpower even after the unfairness of it all has long gone. Still, as humans, we are triggered by the "right / wrong" response. If this is you, try this short exercise and see what happens. Working with a suitably prepared partner, turn to them and let them know that they are right. Be firm, be loud, and even scream it if you like. In fact, the louder you tell them they are right, the chances are greater that they will enjoy hearing it. Check their feelings. What did it feel like for them to be told how right they were? It was good, wasn't it?

Now, watch what happens when the same person tells you that you are wrong. Just saying "you're wrong" at normal conversation volume. Even at this volume, how does it feel hearing you are wrong? Now, let the volume increase, so the other person is shouting at you. What happens now? Time and time again, this can escalate to the point that a real argument breaks out, over what, exactly? Just being told you are wrong. No substance here, no evidence, nothing to show, just by being told you are wrong. Amazing, isn't it?

So, what is going on here? Well, it's our old friend, the mygdala, at play, our inner radar that's constantly scanning for safety.

We've all been in the circumstance where we're having a conversation or discussion that moves to argument, with someone and they're convinced you're wrong about something, even though you know you're right.

It doesn't even matter what; it could be trivial facts or serious issues; how you react to their point of view will likely change the course of the whole conversation.

Here's how. As you read the below, try it out at the same time.

Do your best to avoid becoming emotionally overwhelmed. Your behaviour is an external display of your emotions, and if you get triggered and angry, it's going to show in how you behave. The opposition to your point of view will be processed first through the emotional centres of your brain, leading to an emotional response. This is quite normal, and so far, so good. The next step is to be aware of your emotional state and decide if you are getting a little overheated. If you reframe the discussion or argument as a way of clarifying your thinking, then what could have been a full-blown row could be brought down to a conversation.

People often avoid having difficult conversations as their inner self fears rejection, someone pointing out they are wrong, or a full heated argument. To be fair, there aren't many people who thrive on anger over peace and keeping the peace can be a good thing, but if you are sacrificing something of yourself to keep that peace, it's inauthentic harmony. At some point, there will be an explosion then everything you've tried to keep a lid on will be out and up for discussion. It's better to deal with the unease when it's small and manageable.

The goal here is not to be able to change someone's mind with your point of view, and it is entirely possible that your point of view is missing some key, pivotal information. As *Steven Covey* said in his book *7 Habits of Highly Effective People*, it is far better to seek to understand before you try to be understood. Although let's be clear that some things just are. For example, the Eiffel Tower is 300m tall (324 to the tip), Mount Everest is 8,848m tall, and the world is round. All objective, irrefutable facts. Subjective facts, or opinions, are different, and we do need to be able to distinguish between the two. In the modern era, news is spread very quickly through social media platforms, and we should always be careful to understand that just because we've heard the same "fact" from three or four different sources, it doesn't make that piece of information true. When you are confronted with an opinion that doesn't resonate with you or that you don't like, it's a good idea to remember that it is just an opinion, which in turn is made up of a filtered sense of reality reconfigured in the brain to make sense of and replayed to you in words that describe the event. You then, in turn, accept that description. Through your own filters, you'll make sense of whatever has just been described to you. There are bound to be some grey areas and elements that need some clarification.

How you respond to a "fact" or opinion you hear must also fit into social norms such that, for example, a parent or elder will probably be treated more politely than a politician. A vindictive boss at work will probably be treated differently than your mother. We, therefore, do take a small but significant amount of time to adjust our response, noting all the while our emotional trigger. Often, if triggered negatively, it's good to take a breath here to pause for just a second and respond rather than react immediately. In this way, a discussion becomes just that, a way of clarifying our views openly to make an informed decision.

By going into a potentially heated discussion and keeping calm, you allow yourself a choice of responses. As humans, we have a huge amount of potential, but to access all our wonderful resources, we need to be in the best state possible. When I first heard that, I remember thinking, "of course we do." If I'm angry, how can I think about being anything other than angry? In truth, it takes a little more than a few deep breaths to get rid of anger and be able to access all our inner resources. I've mentioned Coherence Breathing before, and I'll do it again here as it is crucially important. Those few breaths that calm you down are not enough. Coherence is the way forward. It is possible to be angry and calm at the same time, so the shift in mindset is the difference that makes the difference.

If you're not sure what to do, it may be useful to go back a chapter and re-read the exercises, then make them part of your daily routine.

Anxiety takes energy, robbing us of being at our best. When we experience anxiety, our heart speeds up, we sweat, and our muscles tense. Anxiety might be better if it had the decency to burn more calories, but there really isn't an upside. Having a restless mind destroys our focus and concentration and can cause many sleepless nights. A restless mind drains us. Then, when it's time to sleep, it won't turn off.

If your mind is restless, read on for some tips on how to calm it. It takes practice and determination, but the restless mind can absolutely be made calm. Like most hard paths, it's worth it. You will be able to make informed decisions because you won't be in survival mode, and you will be able to relax more.

Cognitive Distancing

The restless mind is trying to protect you. It is warning you of future dangers, but it can get out of control. Realise that your mind is only guessing what might happen; it doesn't know.

Distance yourself from your anxious thoughts. Step back and think about facts. How likely is it that the thing you fear will happen? What can you do to prevent it? Take a deep breath, step back, and make a fact-based plan.

Focus on the Moment

Focusing on the moment is a mindfulness practice that teaches you to get out of your head, out of the past, and out of the future. The restless mind indulges in all kinds of horror fantasies that are not based on reality or the task at hand.

If you focus on the moment, your mind gains tangible facts and details with which to construct your reactions. Your mind will be unable to lose itself in worry if you are focused on a conversation, delicious meal, or game, for instance. So put your mind to work focusing on the moment.

Take Action

There's nothing worse for a restless mind than sitting around.

You can't just take any action, though; you must calculate how to make your life better. You won't be good at it at first, either. You'll need to act like a scientist. Try some things out, evaluate your results, and then try something else. When you see yourself making progress, your mind will calm down.

Don't Indulge Useless Thoughts

In her article *9 Ways to Calm Your Anxious Mind* published in PsychologyToday.com, Melanie Greenberg, PhD, points out that "just because a thought is true doesn't mean that it is helpful to focus on—at least not all the time. If only one in ten people will get the job you seek, for instance, and you keep thinking about those odds, you may become demotivated and not even bother applying."

Your mind identifies trouble so that you can act, not to you convince yourself not to try. We often indulge in a myriad of useless thoughts. Does this person like me enough? Am I doing the right job? Will my car break down? These are vague worries that will not help you in life. They weigh you down, so do not indulge them.

Step Back and Think

Re-evaluation is important for progress. If we don't step back to think every now and then, we keep doing the same things over and over. Insanity, as they say, is doing the same things and expecting different results. So, step back for a minute and think.

When you step back, find a way to measure progress. If you've got fitness goals, you can weigh yourself and decide if you need a better workout. If you've got money goals, evaluate how much you're spending and what you can do to earn more.

You've got this!

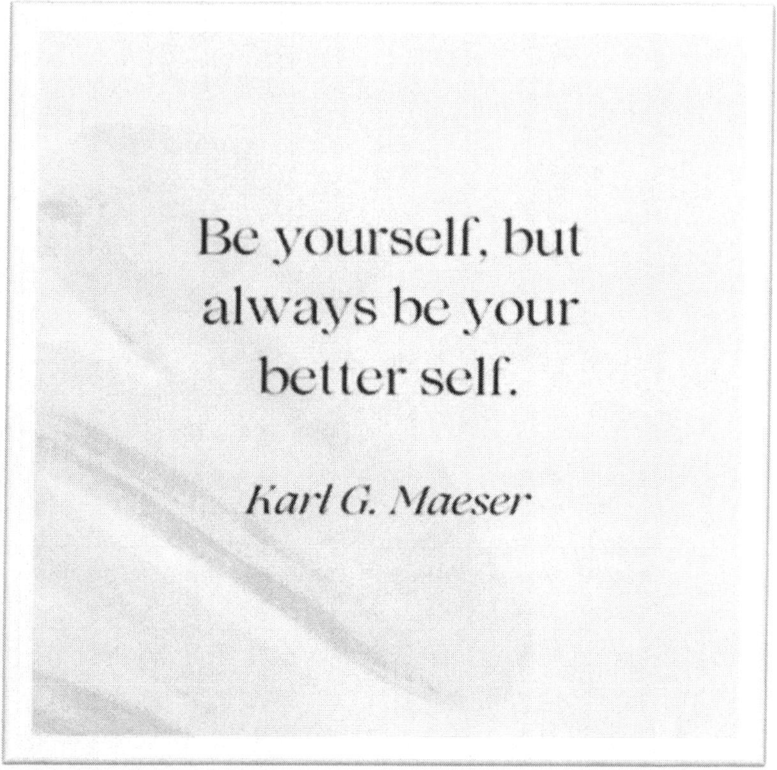
Be yourself, but
always be your
better self.
Karl G. Maeser

CHAPTER 7

Resistance to Change

Being watchful, precautious, and reflective while taking your time to do important things might have advantages, but if your habit is inching more towards procrastination, then it could be that you are resistant to change. And, frankly speaking, you are not alone. Most people are resistant to change to some degree because of the level of uncertainty it brings with it.

Recognising Any Resistance to Change

The truth is that most people hold many assumptions about change. They resist it because it is unknown and therefore frightening. It takes effort to act on changes, and some aren't so keen on putting in that effort. Some don't believe they will see the results they seek, so why try? Others think they don't deserve to be happy, so they don't change to improve their situations. Some get so lost and stuck in a cycle of anxiety that they fail to recognise a scope for change, for a better life. While most of these thoughts are, indeed, assumptions, they can become the very beliefs that stand in the way of what you want to achieve.

Take the quiz below to know if you are resistant to change

Exercise 9 – The Fear of Change Quiz

Check the statements that resonate with your feelings.

- I can take a risk, but what if I fail? Maybe, I should not.
- I can seek help, but what if no one offers? What if I get rejected?
- I always have trouble acting on changes. What if I mess up again?
- What's the point? I always get my hopes up but fail and get disappointed.
- I can't do this. I'll never change. Why try? I don't want to fail again.
- I'm too anxious to succeed.
- Belief-Systems That Stop You from Acting on a Change
- It's better to be realistic and accept my shortcomings. I'm not going to change. I know that.
- I'm not as good as the others. Surely, I can't compete with them.
- I don't want to ask for help. It will make my weaknesses obvious, and then everyone will know.
- I don't think anyone cares. No one will help me.
- I messed up when I could have made things better. That was my only chance. I can't do anything now and must settle for what comes my way.
- Self-Sympathy. Self-Loathe. Anxiety. Depression.
- I am helpless. No one cares, and no one will help.
- I've been misunderstood and mistreated all my life. No one changed for me, so why should I change?
- They don't realise that I don't like being this way, that I have no choice.

- This is so unfair.
- Oh, forget it. I'm hopeless. I hate myself.
- People will mock me. They already are. I know it, and I want to hide.
- There is no point. I can't see any purpose in my life.
- I'm so alone, and I want to cry

What Do You See?

The more checks you have, the more you are resistant to change. While the above statements might not be pleasant to realise about oneself, it isn't entirely your fault if you hold any or many of these blocking beliefs.

People pick these ideas because of the circumstances and experiences they've lived. What's significant is that you can change; we all can. You can change right now, or you can try and fail and try again. Both are normal and positive outcomes. Keep at it because the harder you try and the more you persist, the more likely you're going to become the change.

Worksheet for exercise 9 - Acting on Your Change - Blocking Systems

- From the statements you selected above, write down each of your change-blocking beliefs.
- Write down their justifications. Why do you do them? Introspect and elaborate.
- What are the advantages of changing that belief? What are the disadvantages?
- Weigh them. What scores higher?
- Are your beliefs causing you more harm than good?
- What's stopping you from embracing the change?
- Make a list of small actions to reach the bigger change you seek.
- Work on consistency first. Force yourself to do one action at a time, completely. Do it every time.

The more you work on your consistency, the more habituated your routine will become.

Rewriting Your Life - One Change at a Time

Our minds are capable of wonderful things. They can envision a beautiful life. They can create stories and piece together minute details that together give the story the ending it needs. Use this to your advantage. Talk to your mind. Listen to it too. Establish a relationship with it, and once it feels heard and starts responding, teach it to create positive and inspirational thoughts for you.

Plant the seeds to begin the story. For instance, you want to work on your fitness and want to start a jogging routine every morning. Imagine yourself doing this every day. Imagine your life just as you want it to be.

Remember to be realistic in your narrative, so keep the struggles too, because when you do, you give your mind a heads-up of what might come its way. Think about the success you are going to achieve. Imagine and feel it. These images are powerful building blocks. They can then be picked up by your mind to build and breathe life into your reality. As they say, you dream, and you become.

Steve always has trouble embracing change. He works in a multinational company but has been stuck in the same position for the past 15 years. It's not like he doesn't want a change; he craves a change in his job. He wants to do something new, but he is unwilling to learn and adapt to new methods. As a result, he does what he is told to do and nothing more. Most colleagues his age have jumped a couple or more positions. It bothers him, but he believes he can't do anything about it. He struggles to stay focused and interested at work and hence isn't as effective as the others.

His peers are younger than him, and he thinks that's why they turn out smarter. He also thinks they secretly make fun of him. His college year group are way too high up the ladder to socialise with him anymore, or so he thinks, and he doesn't make any effort to mingle with the younger lads either. As a result of all this, his anxiety has taken an ugly turn.

He's anxious all the time. Fortunately, an old friend notices Steve's behaviour and reaches out to him. He tells him about his resistance to change and how it is stopping him from becoming a better version of himself. Because Steve is at a point when he really wants to change, he listens. He decides to give change a shot. He makes plans and decides to act on them, one change at a time. He also reaches out to his family and other friends for support. They all want to help and do their best to keep him motivated.

Two years down the line, Steve is a completely transformed person. He works harder and smarter and even mingles with his colleagues. He's made plenty of new friends and enjoys his weekends with his family.

He's going to complete his master's from a prestigious university and is looking forward to the new prospects that will bring him. Steve is happy. He hardly feels anxious anymore, and when he does, he knows how to stay on top of it. His family and friends are happy for Steve and love spending time with him.

Well, like Steve, you too can rewrite your current life script.

You can become the change you always wanted to be.

The time is NOW.

> The heart has become a scientifically proven source of intelligence. It communicates and amazingly wide spectrum of information from health and wellness functions to higher qualities like wisdom and compassions.
>
> *The HeartMath Experience*

CHAPTER 8

Building Resilience

Let's consider what resilience is and then apply it to us as humans. I say this as only recently I was in conversation with an HR professional of a global organisation who thought being resilient meant she had to toughen up. For her, it was all about learning to put up with the excessive daily workload she was expected to get through and to be prepared to work hard to do so, without complaining. To her, this resilience stuff was BS and so ultimately irresponsible of employers to demand it of their staff. Luckily, we chatted, and, of course, her misrepresentation of resilience was altered as her understanding of the term changed. The conversation went along these lines:

The word 'resilience' comes from the world of physical science, not biology. If we take the example of a rubber band in an early definition of resilience, it is the capability of a strained body to recover its size and shape after being subjected to adversity or stress. It is one of the reasons people talk about bouncing back after moments of stress. This may be fine when talking about a rubber band, for example, but not so when describing humans. If we bounce back at all, we are never in the same shape. Maybe physically, but our cognition and psychology will have changed in some way as we internalise that experience. We change.

Another way to look at resilience is about keeping calm in the face of adversity and readjusting quickly from a change in circumstances. Again, though, this is looking at something that happens after the event. It's true that highly resilient people seem to cope better with change at work or in their personal life that others seem to find very difficult to deal with, but there is something more about these people that is good to learn about. People seen as more resilient are often more prepared. This is not to say they live their life looking out for the pitfalls, but they have a greater capacity to handle them. It's a bit like having more "fuel" in their resilience tank, if there is such a thing so that when adverse events happen, and they will, they can spend some of this reserve fuel or energy without needing to refuel immediately so that their life can go on. That fuel is, of course, energy, and we are either running fully charged or not. Today, modern hybrid cars have a battery indicator in them, so it's easy to see when those fuel cells need recharging. If the fuel cells get a little low, the engine management system will kick in and pump energy into the battery to recharge it. Building resilience is a bit like that.

You see, after a particularly heavy workload, we do feel tired. It doesn't matter much if your work is physical or mental, doing a lot of whatever hard work is to you will make you tired. People often talk about being wiped out or drained. Often a change of environment can help, but in that moment, you may realise that thinking clearly and making good decisions becomes more of a challenge. Your temper may become shorter, and you may snap at colleagues. Challenging work becomes hard work and less enjoyable.

This feeling of being drained may be a nutritional need. Stopping for a moment, walking around a little to get the blood flowing, and maybe taking a nutritional snack will all help to refuel, but we often need more than that. This helps the physical need. However, building resilience is about the mental need too. So how does it work?

OK, let's go back to the car analogy. Cars need fuel. How fast you use that fuel depends on a couple of things, but probably mostly on how you drive, assuming that the car is well maintained, the tyres are properly inflated, and the wheels are correctly aligned and balanced. So far, so good. The engine is designed to give maximum efficiency in top gear at a certain RPM, 2,000 RPM for my car. I know that by driving in a straight line, as much as the roads and other traffic allow, in top gear at 2,000 RPM, I get maximum fuel efficiency. It's not the fastest way to drive but, on the motorway, it is within the speed limit so long journeys are just great. We cruise along, and it's the same for our minds and bodies. Doing a relatively challenging task without interruptions, where we can focus on what we are doing, is the best use of our fuel and energy. My car loses its fuel economy, using more fuel when I drive around town. Here there are obstacles to avoid like pedestrians, bikes, and buses. We have to stop at red traffic lights and junctions, and when we start again, we tend to accelerate fairly quickly just to get moving again, in a low gear, all of which demands more of the engine and the available fuel. The car's fuel economy drops, and we are no different.

Imagine working in an environment where there is a lot of

change or many interruptions; then we use energy like we are driving around the town. I work with people who are exhausted by change at work which never seems to end. Top that off with some turmoil at home, and energy levels drop quite quickly and the ability to be resilient in the moment disappears. This is the point at which people either explode, and everyone around them wonders what just happened, or they withdraw and hide their true feelings. Examples include working in a call centre with high target sales or in a factory with a relentless production line sending products to pick, pack, and sort. Our resilience becomes challenged.

To make matters worse, our ability to be resilient is further eroded when we try and run and stop at the same time. Do that in your car, and something will give out quite quickly. Maybe the brakes, the clutch, or even the engine. Before long, your car lets you know that it's had enough and it's time to stop. Your body will, too, as a friend of mine found out all too soon. Travelling takes its toll on us even if we are excited to be going on our holidays. If you have to travel for work, the chances are you travel and work at the same time on both legs of the journey. You are still at work, after all. If you travel extensively, things can go wrong. I don't know if you know this feeling, but sometimes I wake up and wonder where I am. Oddly enough, it rarely happens when I am away from home as I probably make a mental note of where I am. It's an odd feeling to wake at two in the morning and wonder where I am, but then rather nice to realise I am where I should be. However, a friend of mine had this experience in a foreign country after travelling way too much. Unfortunately, it took her far too long to realise that she wasn't at home. In fact, she didn't even know what country she was in. This was when she realised she had to stop and get help.

Her mind and body basically put on the emergency brakes, and she had no choice but to stop.

Her resilience, which up to that point had been pretty strong, failed. She was drained and empty, needing many months to recover her physical and mental strength. I'm happy to report that she is now fully back to her previous self, albeit with a renewed sense of self and the capacity to set boundaries.

Time to recharge!

I'm not sure what my friend did in her journey to recovery, but this is what I recommend you do. It has certainly worked for me. In building and maintaining resilience, the key is to manage our energy, both physically and mentally. It takes a bit of practice, but when you get it, it's a great place to be. Part of this energy management is watching where we spend our energy and, as importantly, where not to spend it. Don't waste it and know when you have spent some so you can take a break and replenish it.

According to the research conducted through the HeartMath Institute, there are four primary domains of resilience, and we've touched on most of them. They are physical, emotional, mental, and spiritual. Let's take a brief look as to what these mean.

Physical is just that, your physical strengths and endurance. How many press-ups and squats can you do without complaining (too much)? How physically flexible are you? Can you touch your toes? The emotional domain also looks at flexibility but with emotions. What's your outlook like? Is it positive? How good are you at self-regulation? This is also hooking into the importance of emotional intelligence. For a good amount of resilience, mental flexibility is also desirable. The Clifton StrengthsFinder would call this Adaptability, and NLP would quote the Law of Requisite Variety, both of which are expanded on later in this book. Suffice it to say, mental flexibility is much better for us than a fixed mindset and being "set in our ways". The mental domain also looks at the ability to focus on the task at hand, have a good attention span, and incorporate multiple points of view. The spiritual domain has nothing to do with believing or otherwise in a higher deity or God; rather, it suggests we need some spiritual flexibility - a commitment to values and tolerance of others' values and beliefs. There is a pre-requisite or convenient supposition from NLP that we should respect another person's model of the world. I'll admit that this can be tricky. For the most part, if we believe different things about the same event, maybe we can discuss and seek to understand first. This is my preferred option. However, when the other person's model of the world completely trashes my deeply held values and beliefs, then I have a problem. These are extreme cases, though, and for the majority of people I meet, the tolerances suggested to build resilience are upheld.

With all four domains explored and intact, as they cross over each other, at the centre is coherence: the sweet spot. The challenge is that most of us tend to waste energy, mainly from the emotional domain. Interestingly, a single big outburst of negative emotion, like anger, is better for us in the long run than an "anger leak", or emotional drain.

(HeartMath is a registered trademark of Quantum Intech, Inc. For all HeartMath trademarks go to www.heartmath.com/trademarks)

Unfortunately, there isn't a single daily decision that doesn't first go through the emotional centres of our brain. So-called negative emotions like anger, sadness, fear, hurt, and guilt will use up energy and, if not stopped, will waste our reserves. These negative emotions are also linked to the release of stress hormones which, unfortunately, stay in our system for longer than they are needed. A short burst of cortisol is great, it gets us ready for whatever we need to escape from, but when released, other systems shut down, including the blood flow to the periphery, the alimentary canal, and our immune system. These systems don't stop altogether, but they are certainly reduced. Prolonged exposure to cortisol can have a negative and detrimental effect on our entire system. The big challenge for today's workforce is that with such an increase in demand and information exchange, our stress baseline gets reset by the baroreceptors in the heart, reading this heightened level of cortisol as the new "normal". The damage has started.

Through building resilience and readdressing this balance into a more positive state, we can reset the baroreceptors to a lower setting as the levels of circulating cortisol decline.

Don't worry; the cortisol release will still be there when you need to jump out of the way for safety but will stop being fired off just because your boss looks at you strangely.

> *"It's easy to forget that stress is one of your body's warning signals that tells you something is out of whack. If you ignore those signals, especially your emotions, you could become so accustomed to the situation of stress, ongoing tension and strain that stress can start to seem normal. When a lot of people in a particular environment are stressed, they can create a climate that makes it more difficult for any one person to see his or her own stress clearly. When you have a whole culture pushing high performance, sometimes people don't want to admit it or address it"* — Henry J Kan, M.D.

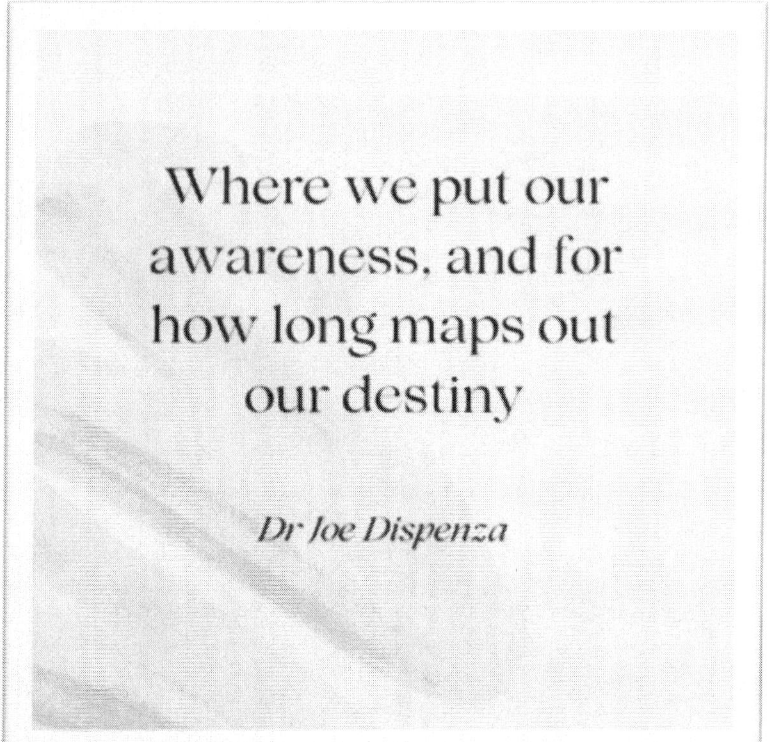
Where we put our
awareness, and for
how long maps out
our destiny
Dr Joe Dispenza

CHAPTER 9

Managing your Stress

Stress is often brought on by anxiety, and when this condition is addressed, it is possible to avoid building up stress levels within an individual's daily functions. Addressing the underlying causes of the stress would better help the individual deal with or change the circumstances that caused the stress and thereby learn to comfortably adapt and cope with workplace situations.

The following are some recommendations on how to manage stress at work effectively:

- Give up coffee or maybe reduce your intake by one or two cups. Most people are unaware of the effect coffee has on the body and mind systems. Coffee helps to elevate any existing conditions into hyperactivity, thus creating the ideal combination to further enhance any stressful circumstances. Caffeine flows into the blood and causes adrenaline to be overly stimulated, thus putting the brain into overdrive.

- Be better organised is another popular piece of advice given to most stress-filled individuals. The idea of being organised does not seem to have any clear positive contributions to the individual and, therefore, the inability to incorporate this very beneficial trait into a daily schedule. Learning the benefits of being organised will help a stressed-out individual better appreciate its positive contributing factors, and when this is well incorporated as a daily practice, their quality of life will definitely be much better.

- Taking short breaks to stretch and relax the mind periodically will also help to keep stress under control. Whenever someone feels a little pressured, taking a few minutes to unwind and refocus after being energised will be helpful. Getting some fresh air will also work wonders on the body and mind.

- Stopping for lunch and tea breaks is also very important to take the mind off work for a little while. Taking time to enjoy the break while the body goes through the replenishment of nutrients is also a good idea.

- The home environment can usually seem like a battlefield as there are usually individuals of various ages under one roof. This alone is a stress contributing factor, as there are many needs and wants to satisfy and cope with. With some correct and comfortable practices, the stress levels for all concerned can be minimised.

The following are some of the common areas that should be given due consideration in the quest to limit the occurrences of stress:

Being organised is probably the best way to beat the stress condition from being a regular occurrence. When there is some form of organisation evident, all the individual elements that contribute to a smoother flow in a day would be covered, thus unfolding a completely new and calmer way of getting through the day.

It is recommended to take the time to relax during a hectic day using whatever activities most suit the individual. These may include meditation, prayer, light exercise, or deep breathing exercises, all of which contribute to rejuvenating the mind and body to face the rest of the home front issues.

People who have the time to incorporate an exercise regimen before the start of the day's main activities have attested to the fact that the body and mind are better able to cope with the onslaughts of the day, which include managing home problems. Stress at home can be avoided with this good start to the day, as it's refreshing and energising.

Talking to people with similar issues could help an individual to learn and practise some activities that others incorporate into their lives and home environment, and this may help eliminate the stress-causing circumstances. Trying different ways to handle stress at home would be a better way to cope as opposed to just keeping things repressed which will only end up contributing to higher stress levels.

A good number of problems with a relationship can be sorted out easily by tackling the key issues that usually bring forth these problems. However, when these key issues are not addressed and dealt with, the occurrence of stress becomes the norm, and this is a rather unpleasant and potentially damaging situation.

The following are some issues that often bring out stress conditions, and by managing these elements well, the individual will be able to enjoy a better-quality relationship:

Both parties should be made aware of the fact that it is almost always impossible to change someone overnight or even over a long period. Accepting this is the first step in managing a relationship without adding stress to the combination.

Working toward coping with an existing situation instead of trying to force a change will be a lot easier and certainly less stressful. Changing oneself is definitely more doable than attempting to change someone else.

People are not naturally mind readers and expecting the other party to be able to feel, read, and understand everything their partner is going through without talking would be very unreasonable indeed.

When this is a common practice, the party who is at a disadvantage because they are unable to read the relationship signs would then become very stressed out when discontent and quarrels start. Therefore, stressing the need to competently voice one's mind and thought process clearly is something that should be regularly practised within the boundaries of the relationship.

Sometimes, the practice of writing down thoughts about a relationship will help put things in a better perspective. All parties will be better able to deal with situations if everything is clearly visible and understood.

For me, the biggest piece of advice I could share is to just listen. Truly meet the other person where they are without judgement. Listen without thinking of a reply. Listen to connect, appreciate and be curious. A lot of people really struggle here because listening is hard. Just think about it. How many times have you been in a conversation where you can see the person you are talking to is ready to bust in with their contribution even before you have finished what you are saying? This very scenario happened to me in a senior executive's office as we were discussing progress with one of his direct reports. I was giving a summary of my feedback, and he was looking at me like a goldfish gasping for air. His mouth would pop open as if ready to speak, but I carried on. I mean, I hadn't finished what I was saying. Eventually, it got too much for me, and I stopped and told him that I could see he was ready to share his thoughts with me about what I was saying even before I had finished what I was saying.

There was a moment of silence where I truly thought I was about to get kicked off-site, but, to his credit, he said I was right, that he'd been told about this before, and please carry on, and he would listen.

Do practice active listening. You'll be all the better off for it and, who knows, you might even learn something new.

If introspection and mindfulness can help you understand the origins and outcomes of your stress and anxiety, changing your behaviour can help you overcome them. Read on to see how you can have that experience for a lifetime. By setting goals, you can change your narrative. And by changing what you do, you can change the way you feel.

Evading Avoidance

If you experience fear and anxiety, you probably avoid the things that make you feel uncomfortable. For instance, if you don't like crowds or if socialising makes you feel anxious, then you may choose to avoid crowds like not going out on a holiday or shopping during peak times.

Yes, this might be the most natural thing to do, but here's the problem. Avoidance increases or intensifies anxiety. You may not realise it, but when you avoid something because of fear, the relief of not having to deal with your fear is your biggest reward. It's addictive too. So, if this time you feared large crowds, by avoiding the fear, you decreased your threshold to that fear.

Because of this instant reward, you're more likely to avoid it again. If large crowds make you uncomfortable, soon, smaller crowds will begin to do the same. With time, your avoidance will push you to a point where the mere sight of people or the thought of engaging in the slightest conversation might bring on a panic attack. Identifying and acting against your fears will help you overcome the fear as well as any anxiety that might have accompanied it. With plenty to benefit you, it makes sense to try.

Exercise 10 - Identifying Your Fears

To face your fears, you must first know exactly what you fear. What troubles you the most? What builds your stress? What accelerates your anxiety?

- Reflect on your top five fears - the ones that are getting in the way of your goals and the ones you want to do something about.
- Where do they come from? What situations and events bring on these fears?
- What's the worst that can happen? Imagine it. Describe it in words
- Take your time, and don't rush through the experience.
- Review your answers when you are ready.

Acting against Your Fears

Congratulations. You've completed the first step. You're doing great. Now that you've zeroed in on your fears and where they come from, you can create a plan to overcome them.

Exercise 11 - Taking the Step-Up Approach

Pick the least feared item from your checklist.

Create steps that will help you overcome your fear, for example:

- Take time to reflect on your plan; keep it real and in order.
- Take small steps to execute your plan and face your fear, tracking your progress until the fear doesn't bother you anymore.
- Again, don't rush; take your time to adjust to the experience and embrace the changes that come with it.

Begin the Process: Create and Execute Your Plan

Great, so you've tapped into your strengths, recognised what you want, and laid out goals that will keep you busy. What next? Well, you could create a formidable plan to materialise these deliverables.

Your ability to set up a quick, direct, and foolproof action plan for your goals is what is going to see you through to the finish line. If you walk into the game with just the right cards in your pocket, you've got yourself a winner from the very beginning.

Consider Every Aspect That Might Influence, Conflict or Jeopardise Your Plan

Brainstorm a properly written plan that lists out the specific details of your action steps and deadlines. There is no such thing as an ideal plan; your plan is only as good as your thoughts are today.

The more you learn, the more your plan is likely to change. Take time to prioritise your action steps and the sequence they are likely to follow. Treat it as the blueprint of your road to success. The more groundwork you invest in it, the more foolproof and success-oriented it becomes.

Be Mindful of Any possible Setbacks, But Don't Let Them Wear You Down

What if an old fear comes back? What if I get stressed out all over again? What if the anxiety comes back? Will it come back?

The truth is, we don't know. Everyone's anxiety and experience are different. However, you now know how to get on top of them. Don't let the fear of evoking a fear drain you. You have better things to focus on. Stay positive.

No Need to Hurry

Remember, while this might be about achieving your goals, it is also about overcoming your anxiety. You do not want to create a situation where you've bitten off more than you can chew. You're in this for a lifetime, and it's always going to be work-in-progress. Have some self-compassion and know that each day, you're better than what you were yesterday.

Know When You've Tried Too Long

Because anxiety forces your thought process to be rigid, it can sometimes make you persist on tasks even when you know they aren't working out. Recognise the signs that you need to stop persisting.

It's OK to Fall. To Fail Too

No one is perfect, and there is no ideal plan. Keep asking yourself what's working and what isn't? If you think you're missing the bus and there's scope for improvement, don't be ashamed to go back to the drawing board and start again. You'll be surprised by the wave of new ideas coming your way.

Realign Your Plan. Improvise Too

Always ask yourself, "Is there a better way around?" When you stay open to new ideas, you make room for creativity and growth.

Complete What You've Taken

Uncertainty can trigger a degree of anxiety in most people, but for a person suffering from anxiety, any sense of uncertainty, whether it comes from a space of unfinished tasks or repeated failures, can trigger the worst symptoms. Your anxious mind is probably waiting for a chance to bounce back in and take control, which it will inevitably try to do.

The key is to be aware of this but not get perturbed by it. Complete what you've started and only move ahead when you've finished your previous task. The joy of seeing through a project from start to end will give you the confidence to win over anxiety for good.

Become a Better Version of You

Once you've created your plan and find it executing rather well, it's time you reach out for brighter and more rewarding pastures. You've worked hard to make it so far, and now, it's time to capitalise on your achievements and make advancements. Experiment with ideas and invent new ones. Be a game-changer. When you've channelled your energies in the right place and know you have things going for you, there will be no room for anxiety or fear to enter your life.

Anxiety happens when you think you have to figure out everything at once. Breathe. You're strong. You've got this. Take it day by day.

Karen Salmansohn

CHAPTER 10

Why Emotional Intelligence Matters

Emotional intelligence as we know it today has been shaped mainly by the psychologist and New York Times science writer Daniel Goleman's 1995 book *Emotional Intelligence: Why It Can Matter More Than IQ*. However, his work had been built on others as far back as the 1930s when the concept of social intelligence was described by Edward Thorndyke. Emotional intelligence (or emotional quotient or EQ) has been a while in the making and is only today being recognised by many corporations as the difference that makes the difference in great leaders.

But what has EQ got to do with managing your levels of stress and clearing your head in the moment when all about are losing theirs? To understand the answer to this question, let's first take a brief look at what EQ is.

A common definition is that emotional intelligence is the ability to identify and manage your emotions and the emotions of others. It is generally said to include three skills: emotional awareness, the ability to harness emotions and apply them to tasks like thinking and problem solving, and the ability to manage emotions, including regulating your emotions and cheering up or calming down other people.

One expert and someone who I trained with Dr. Martyn Newman, PhD, built on the shoulders of giants like Dan Goleman and Reuven Bar-On to understand what great leaders do in terms of EQ. What behaviours do they have that make them great, and how do these behaviours work as EQ competencies? Through his work, today, we have ten clearly identifiable competencies that can be learned, and that can help you keep your head clear of noise to focus on the task at hand.

In the context of this book, the full list isn't as important as the couple that makes the difference in managing stress and anxiety. I do, however, recommend discovering more about your EQ and how you can develop it to master your state. With this in mind, let's look at emotional awareness and, specifically, self-awareness, which Martyn Newman segmented into straightforwardness and self-knowing.

By way of a working definition, Martyn Newman explains, in his book Emotional Capitalists : The New Leaders, that people who are high in self-knowing are aware of their emotional experiences and know what they are feeling most of the time. They have the capacity to recognise how their feelings and emotions impact their personal opinions, attitudes, and judgments. It's also the platform on which most other aspects of EQ rest.

If you are good at self-knowing, the chances are you are someone who can recognise the impact of your behaviour on other people. You're going to be good at putting into words what you are thinking and, importantly, feeling and recognise that you can modify the way in which you express yourself and the behaviour you show when it is appropriate to do so. As such, your non-verbal communication (body language) can be easy for others to read, such that the words you use and the non-verbal communication you display are congruent, leaving no one in doubt about your authenticity.

Easy, isn't it?

Well, maybe not so.

Trouble in the moment and when our stress levels rise tend to be due to distractions. Too many distractions could cause us to question our productivity. Are we being as productive as we might or should be? (By the way, that word "should" is the topic in the next chapter). This worry we generate about our own contribution generates less focus and feeds that cycle in ever-decreasing circles. This may sound logical, but most of us don't even recognise we are doing this until it's too late and we become completely overwhelmed, drained, unable to focus or concentrate, and exhausted.

A key reason people get burned out is their lack of awareness of their emotional intelligence and, in particular, self-knowing. Awareness will help enormously. It is why some people cope better than others in highly demanding jobs.

By developing your self-knowing, you will notice a few things like:

Starting to tune in to your physical sensations and become aware of the feelings you are experiencing as you face new challenges in work and outside of work. As mentioned before, we are creatures of habit, and as such, partly down to doing similar actions repeatedly, we have stopped recognising the emotional impact of our behaviour. Every decision we make is based on emotions, and we need to get back to acknowledging and becoming aware of the prevalent emotion as our mind and body start to sense its presence.

Maybe understanding our Emotional Landscape or Depletion to Renewal grid, as HeartMath® would call it, could be useful. You see, the thing about emotions is that they are brought on by feelings, which in turn are brought from our physiological state. Our behaviour is affected by the environment we are experiencing. If that environment is full of fear and unknown or yet to be expressed aggression from, for example, a political leader, it would be usual to live a life in fear, an emotion that depletes us and wears down our inner battery. You will hear people tell you that they feel tired of the situation, worn out by the negativity that is going on. Fear, along with anxiety and anger, puts us in a state of depletion. Our heart rate is elevated, and we release cortisol into our bloodstream to do... well, all the things that cortisol does without running away.

Our subconscious mind is highly imaginative and creative and, as such, has a lot of difficulties distinguishing what is real from what is imagined. So, regardless of bombs dropping, a truly horrific fight or flight scenario, the mere thought that they could is enough to trigger the response. Knowing this, we must also know that our emotions are in our control. No one can make you angry without a huge amount of permission from yourself, so it is that providing we acknowledge our emotional state, we have the power to change it to a different state that can renew us and recharge those depleted batteries.

A physiological thing we can do to override our subconscious mind controls the rate of our breathing. We can speed it up and hyperventilate (not recommended) or slow it down and calm down. However, calming down isn't enough. We can be calm and still, depleting our inner resources, and I've had clients say to me that when they acknowledge their anger and shift to calm down, they are left with sadness. It's true that emotions like sadness, guilt, and boredom can be associated with a lower heart rate, so being calm but still releasing cortisol. It's not the cortisol that raises the heart rate but the adrenaline that is released alongside it for the fight or flight response. In this state, we are still depleting. The shift to renewal comes after we check-in and acknowledge we are in a depleting state. This isn't about ignoring the anger or sadness but acknowledging it and moving it to something that supports you and switches off the cortisol.

In a high heart rate situation, we can shift anxiety to excitement. Neurologically these two states follow very similar pathways, and physiologically, they send similar sensations to the body, so it's down to a choice as to whether we enjoy and are excited by the roller coaster ride or find it a horrific experience never to be repeated. In this area, we can experience emotions like excitement, passion, joy and so on, all of which are associated with a raised heart rate, but instead of cortisol, we start to release DHEA, dehydroepiandrosterone, also known as the youth hormone. These days you can buy it via the wonders of the internet, but why bother when you can make a mental switch and produce your own, for free, without any undesirable side effects. Interestingly the precursor of cortisol and DHEA is the same, pregnenolone, so we can, to some extent, switch off the cortisol production and start producing DHEA to redress the balance.

It gets better. Other renewing states come with a lower heart rate, and this is where the magic truly happens. I mentioned earlier that one of the things we can do to override our subconscious mind is deliberately playing with our breathing rate. Having now become aware of your emotions, you're encouraged to move deeper into becoming more aware of how your thoughts shape your feelings and, ultimately, your behaviour.

What is causing you to feel stressed or anxious? To deal with the stress, we need to understand what is triggering the response in us. This is a time for some self-reflection and making a list of all the things in your life that you consider are causing you stress. In that list will be some things that you can control and others that might seem out of your control. Notice what the environment is like when stress is triggered compared to times when it is not. Who is around you, and so on? Once done, it's time to see what you can do to change the things you can change.

As mentioned before, we are creatures of habit, so when you notice your focus shifting, stop and ask yourself what happened. What are the patterns of thought or action that you went through to shift your focus away from the task at hand? Only by knowing and understanding these patterns or habits will you be able to break that pattern and do something more productive instead by laying down a new pattern to follow. Sharpening your focus takes some time to develop, and the first step is to become aware of what happens when you lose it.

We can start to circumnavigate this challenge by setting very good and specific intentions from the outset. When starting a new task, or project, ask yourself what you want to achieve with this. Be as specific as you can, as the more specific you are, the greater the chance you will deliver. Add into this mix how you feel when you have achieved what you set out to achieve, again being very specific to the point that you write down everything you will see, everything you will hear, and everything you will feel when you reach this goal. Who will be with you, where will you be etc.?

And finally, for now, close your eyes and clear your mind

(remember the breathing pattern). Focus on your breath and get back to balanced breathing to the count of 5 or 6 in and 5 or 6 out for a minute or two. Make this a new habit every time your awareness signals that you've been triggered. Once your breathing is slowed, focus your attention on the heart area of your chest. Imagine, if you can, that your breath is coming in and leaving you through this area. Yes, it takes a leap in the imagination, but it's worth getting into. This will, after a few breaths, slow your heart rate down, and you will experience calm. Having done this for a few breaths, change your state. The goal is to move away from the anger or sadness and out of the excitement and passion into a renewing state of ease, care, and appreciation. A lot of people find it easier to step into a state of gratitude, so why not try that too?

I'll be honest with you here, it's not necessarily easy to do, but once you feel that state come in, it's definitely worth it!

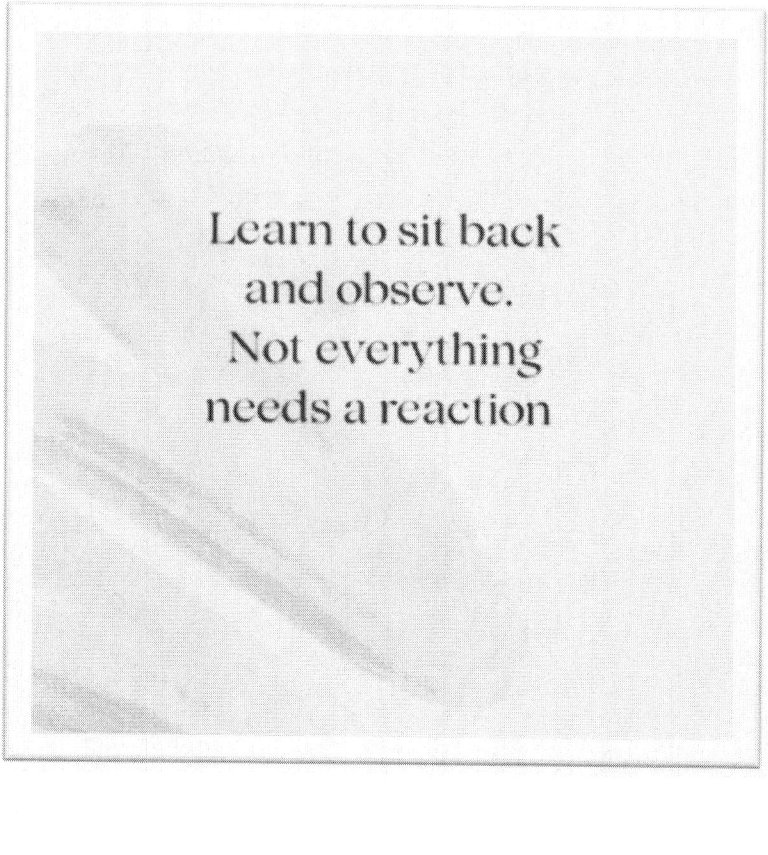
Learn to sit back
and observe.
Not everything
needs a reaction

CHAPTER 11

Our Inner Self Talk

Is your inner dialogue chaotic?

Have you ever tuned out of a conversation because you're more involved in the discussion going on in your head? Did you find yourself getting irritated at someone droning on because it's distracting you from that argument raging within you?

You're not alone in feeling as though your inner dialogue is chaotic. Instead of constantly trying to drown things out, you find yourself turning everything down. All you want is to indulge those chaotic thoughts. You convince yourself that by arguing it out, you'll come to a solution, but instead, you find yourself at an impasse.

The reality is that most people are fuelled by the voice in their head, that non-stop stream of thoughts. It's worth noting that the most negative thoughts seem to come through loud and clear, while the positive ones whisper too quietly for you to make them out.

Often, that inner dialogue is humiliating. It's panic-ridden and defeatist. It wants to tear you down, drag you out, and leave you to suffer. It's tumultuous, creating chaos in your mind. Your inner dialogue is driving your life, and where do you think you're heading if you're being driven by chaos and negativity? It's tough, but the only way to pull through it is to stay calm and override the chaos.

Where does this voice come from? It's built from birth. You absorb the tones of a teacher, the exasperated chiding from an angry parent, or the put-downs of an unkind older sibling. All these external influences shape your inner dialogue.

Unfortunately, we often absorb the negativity and allow it to take a prominent position, drowning out any positive voices trying to whisper in our ears. This is especially true when an authority figure repeats this message, and it gets lodged in your inner dialogue.

The only way to counter this chaotic inner dialogue is by changing the way you think. This is an active task that you must undertake with intention. If you set about intentionally changing how you think and speak to yourself, you will notice a change in your self-confidence, self-esteem, and self-worth. Your inner dialogue can build you up, or it can tear you down.

It's difficult to flip the script. It's easier to fall back on the negative voice of a parent berating you for something you might have done when you were seven than it is to nurture the positive voice of that same parent praising you for something the same day. The brutish voices rise above the chaos and speak the loudest, and the kind tone and words somehow fade into the background.

What causes chaotic inner dialogue? In addition to the past shaping it, it is often driven by stress. It manifests in chaotic, bullying inner dialogue. We feel a sense of injustice, for whatever reason, and it's difficult to overcome that when the blows keep coming.

So, how can you tell whether your inner dialogue is truly chaotic? A good test would be to look at your life. Is it chaotic? Is it making you miserable? Do you feel unhappy with your actions, thoughts, words, and choices? If so, there's a good chance your inner dialogue is chaotic. If you "shush" people so you can retreat to the arguments in your head, or if you struggle to focus on tasks because those voices are too loud, then your inner dialogue is chaotic.

It doesn't have to be. It's possible to change your inner dialogue to a more positive tone. It takes a lot of practice, and you will need to consistently correct it with positive thoughts and affirmations. You should also enlist some stress management techniques to help calm your emotions to further control them.

So, let's go right back to where it all started. Was it at the moment of conception or before that? There is a school of thought that believes we are not just the product of our biological parents. A theory suggests that unresolved memories with negative emotions attached to them from the past are handed on through the DNA for up to three generations. It's not really the topic of this book, but there have been people in my consulting room who, when releasing the challenges of their great grandparents, found the stress and anxiety they were currently experiencing were released too. That said, I have helped some people who, when asked if they knew whether the first event of their current challenge was before, during, or after their birth, said before. It's not my job to challenge them, and if that's what comes up, we go with it.

For most people, we discuss the time after their birth, and it's well known today that as we are born, we are pretty much a blank canvas. Our heart is fully formed, but our brain is far from useful. In fact, the only functioning part of the brain is the reptilian brain, with other parts coming on board as we mature. The brain fully matures at about age 25. That's quite some time, isn't it? In all that time, we are being programmed and reprogrammed, first from our parents or caregivers, then later from school, universities, and life experiences. We learn how to get what we need to survive and thrive; we learn how to communicate with our parents and teachers learning the social rules of engagement along the way. We may even learn a second or third language and all things scientific, from basic chemistry and biology to the language of mathematics and physics. All these facts help us mostly discern fact from fiction). We start to understand the subtleties of non-verbal communication and the tone of the spoken and then written word, ultimately learning how to "read between the lines" of whatever is being communicated to us.

In our early formative years, though, we set up patterns of behaviours and beliefs about ourselves that don't necessarily help us when we are older. Take, for example, my client, who we'll call Annie. While we discussed how she felt stress, what stressed her out, and what her coping mechanisms were, she stated quite boldly that she was not lovable—quite an admission. She went on to describe failed relationship after failed relationship that always ended with her backing out. She was protecting herself from being hurt and yet, ironically, was hurting herself with her lack of trust.

As young children, we lack the capacity to critique. I'm not talking about critiquing what we are experiencing; I'm talking about having that critical faculty that helps make some sense of what we are witnessing without taking it personally. So, for example, a three-year-old child might see their parents arguing over, well, anything, and usually something trivial. Parents of young children are often sleep-deprived, which lowers their threshold for keeping calm and raises the opportunity for arguing. Anyway, whatever the parents are arguing over, the three-year-old child is not capable of watching and thinking, "Oh, look, there is one adult human trying to impose their values and beliefs on another adult human, and the second human is not accepting them and is displaying some anger at the very idea that they should".

No, what the three-year-old child sees is their primary caregivers, from whom they want and expect love, making an almighty din which, as a three-year-old child, they take upon themselves. "If my parents are arguing, it must be my fault."

Something similar happened to Annie. As a very young child, she remembered wanting her father's love, and yet, for some reason, her father was not capable of showing that love for his daughter. Instead of Annie thinking, "Oh, my poor dad is unable to give me love or maybe even feel love for his own child, possibly down to how he was brought up by his emotionally vapid parents or during a time of immense hardship for the entire family" she blamed herself. Every time.

When you can see this reasoning as an adult, it makes sense, and now, as an adult, Annie was able to rationalise these past events that kept her locked into the notion that she was not lovable, those patterns of behaviour that reinforced the decision she took all those years ago to be unlovable.

The thing is, we all have them and they surface at the oddest times. Once we realise that our belief was formed a long time ago, in a time in our life when we had little control of our thoughts, we then collect evidence to support the experience as being correct, and there you have it. A pattern of behaviour, or strategy, that conditions our response and other strategies as we grow. It's a little like building a house fit for a four-year-old on foundations that are OK when we are four but not supporting the house we need when we are 34.

Another key inner self-talk is known as Parts. I find it fascinating that people can describe what's happening in their world and what's generating their stress and not hear what they say. A case in point happened when, on the same day, two clients talked to me about their recent experiences and aspirations, and both mentioned the phrase "part of me" six times in a minute. You know the kind of thing, part of me wants to go live in Australia but part of me doesn't, or part of me wants that cake, but part of me knows I shouldn't. Whenever we talk about ourselves and include this phrase, it suggests an inner conflict or incongruence. The interesting thing for me with these two clients was that neither had heard themselves say it. Six times in a minute, and they hadn't heard it! This was interesting as this inner conflict is also something that will drive a stress response and release of cortisol. By vocalising the part, and the self-limiting belief, the client has an opportunity to get to the root of the problem or challenge they are facing and, thus, a chance to update their inner operating system, like their iOS, to form a new belief or resolve the parts. For Annie, understanding what was going on and why her father might have behaved the way he did allowed her to see and believe that it wasn't her fault. This understanding led her to accept and move on to a fulfilling and lasting relationship, something she really didn't think could happen.

The clients with the parts also had transformational moments, as is often the case, as the parts in the conflict tend to sound like someone they knew. Again, these parts are often formed years before and, once exposed, talked about, and understood, the parts resolve themselves leading to better, clearer decisions allowing the person to move on happily with their life.

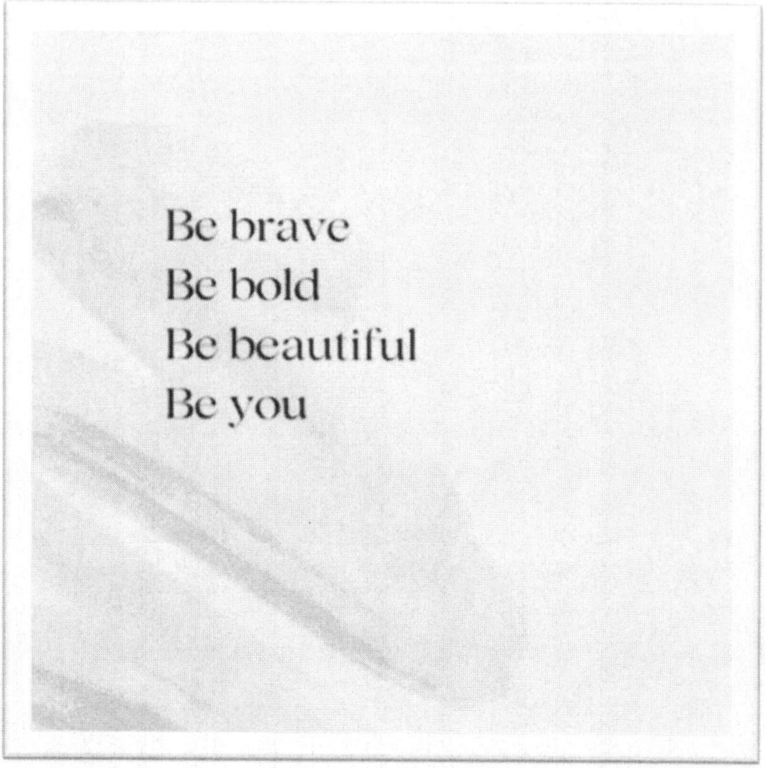
Be brave
Be bold
Be beautiful
Be you

CHAPTER 12

From Stress to Strength

There's a lot to be said for focussing on what you're good at and leaving the rest up to those that thrive in their area of talent. Some of our modern-day stresses come from having to continue to do what we are doing, supporting our family or lifestyle, even if we don't like it or, worse, hate it.

In writing this book, I interviewed many people who were doing just that. They were functioning in a job that was OK but not fulfilling, a job they'd been trained or educated to do but didn't enjoy. They were also, mostly, very well rewarded by their company for doing their job, but every one of them hated Monday mornings. If you could be passionate about hating, they would be. In fact, that feeling started on Sunday. I've got to admit this was me, too, although I was luckier than some of those I interviewed. One thing I have been good at in my life is trusting my intuition, and, in this way, I could escape before I fell.

Not so for Mary.

The stress impact on Mary's life led to a breakdown and six

months away from her employer. One day, she woke up as normal, got out of bed, and fell to the floor. Her body said, "No more". Mary's gruelling workload had finally caught up with her, and she had to stop. She couldn't move. She was forced to stop. Now, while this may sound melodramatic, it's happening around us, and if we don't take care of ourselves and watch out for the signals and listen to what our body is saying, this could happen to us.

It took Mary a week to be diagnosed and signed off work to go home and recuperate. The company she worked with was compassionate and supported her during her recovery, but even so, she told me it took her a full two years before she could say "I'm back", that is, back to the full capacity and energy levels she had before her collapse. During that time, Mary was able to reflect and focus on what she was doing and what she really wanted out of her life. One thing that changed immediately was starting to manage her time and work the hours she was being paid for. She doesn't work overtime, although should the job demand it during times of high demand, she gets her time back, not money. She's also reconnected with some of her talents that slipped away while she was building her career, talents that are actually strengths.

We all have them. According to the Gallup Organisation, a talent is a naturally recurring pattern of thought, feeling, or behaviour that can be productively applied. Talents, knowledge, and skills, along with the time you spend (i.e., investment) practising, developing skills, and building your knowledge base, combine to create your strengths.

So, they are naturally occurring and innate. They are just something you can do, like paint, draw, dance, play the guitar, or cook. Your talents may not be present today, but maybe as a child, you remember loving being out in the woods, building with Lego blocks (other building blocks are available), putting on puppet shows for the local kids, or organising fundraisers for charities. Whatever it is, do you still do some of that now, as an adult? Did you lose your talent in your job, or are you lucky enough to be able to express your talent in your job? The thing about talents is that, when applied consistently to the point that they provide near-perfect performance in a specific activity, they become your strengths.

Although talents, skills, and knowledge are significant for building a strength, talent is always the most important. The reason is that your talents are innate and cannot be acquired, unlike skills and knowledge. For example, as a salesperson, you can learn your products' features (knowledge), you can be trained to ask the right open-ended questions (skill), and you can practise making a sale (investment). However, the innate tendency to push a customer to commit at exactly the right moment, in exactly the right way, must be naturally occurring and cannot be learned.

The key to building a fully developed strength is identifying your most dominant talents, which are likely found within your top five themes, then complementing them with acquired knowledge, skills, and investment.

Through their own research and analysis, Gallup has revealed that people who use their strengths every day are three times more likely to report having an excellent quality of life, six times more likely to be engaged at work, eight per cent more productive, and 15 per cent less likely to quit their jobs.

Mary rediscovered her love of watercolour painting. During her recovery phase and with time on her hands, she started to paint again, taking lessons to help her rekindle her joy of painting and quickly got to a good standard. Figuring out that she had messed up her "work-life" balance (by the way, there is no work-life balance, there is only life), she is now planning a one-woman exhibition. Coupled with her love of travel, she now has the time to put the two talents together and is well on the way to developing this into a strength.

This is all well and good, but can you apply your talents in the workplace, and if so, what does that look like?

Well, the answer to that is a resounding "Yes!" People who have taken the assessment will know that, along with a description of your Top5 talents (or maybe all 34), you will have a description of how these Top5 have been influenced by the way you have approached the full StrengthsFinder assessment. You will have a description of how you might apply those Strength Themes, and there is the juice. While reading this description, some sentences will leap off the page at you as you realise that "Yes, that's me!" You will then be well on your way to describing yourself through your strengths and working with them. The more you figure out where you get your energy from and what takes your energy away, the more likely you are to have an enjoyable working life that sustains you rather than drains you.

You will be moving from Stress to Strength!

However, there is a caveat to working on your strengths. It could appear that by working on our strengths, we are ignoring our weaknesses, but this isn't so. Some of the most stressful experiences in my corporate roles were when I was expected to perform way outside of my strength zone, so much so that I couldn't dig into my strength to refocus my activities. Gallup uses a nice definition of weakness, namely anything that gets in the way of you getting what you want. My most stressful time at work was planning a one-time event over seven sites on four different continents. My top strength theme is 'Adaptability', which is pretty useful as going with the flow is something I needed during the development of this event. Requests for posters from the seven sites were interpreted differently despite sending out guidelines and templates, people worked behind the scenes creating things that weren't communicated, and I became increasingly anxious. This one-time event was to be attended by not only the CEO of our company but also the Chairman. It was a big one. Oh... and we had no budget.

Now, while my Adaptability was in overdrive, my Maximiser, at number five, kept me awake as I figured out a better way to work what we'd done, and there was more and more detail to check. My stress levels and blood pressure were unhealthily high.

The good news is the event was a success, with a key senior leader noting that I was "pivotal to its success", which was nice. But it was a warning to me that planning isn't a strength I've ever had or wished to develop. It drains me, and there I was, once again being put on a project planning course to improve this skill I lacked. In my career, I'd been on two previous project planning courses, and this one, while interesting in the moment, did little to improve my desire to be a project planner. In fact, I can safely say I went from being dreadful at planning projects to be even worse and wasted a lot of productive time learning how to be really bad in the process.

The point is to focus on what you're good at and get to be the best at it you can. In doing so, your head remains clear of distraction and can focus on the good stuff—the stuff that brings you energy, the stuff that drives you out of bed on a Monday morning instead of dreading the day and week ahead.

If you overplay a strength, this can evolve into a weakness

and get in the way of you delivering on your goals. One, in particular, jumps out for me as I've noticed it time and time again. It's the strength theme of Responsibility.

This theme is a tricky one for most people who have it. In the workplace setting, most people with Responsibility seem to abdicate the need to be responsible for themselves first. It works a bit like this. They are working normally at their desk or workstation, and someone, probably more junior to themselves, comes along and asks for help. This is the first warning for anyone with this theme because what they all seem to do is stop what they are doing and deliver the help that has been asked for, there and then. After all, they feel responsible and do what comes naturally to them.

Now, I'm not saying giving help is wrong; I'm saying that as they stop their work to help someone else in need, they increase their workload and will, in nearly all cases I know of, stay late in the office to catch up on what they were doing before they got interrupted. Their time management is disrupted and sacrificed for the needs of others. While this may not be an issue if it happens now and then but over time, it certainly builds up, and stress levels increase with it. Sometimes it's just not possible to stay late, so the work gets taken home to be completed when the kids have gone to bed. None of this is sustainable. So, people who are high in Responsibility do need to check their needs are being met before going to the rescue of a colleague asking for help. Give help; we all need help from time to time, but give it when it suits you rather than right there and then.

Be responsible for yourself first, and in that way, you will ensure you can turn up and be there for others too.

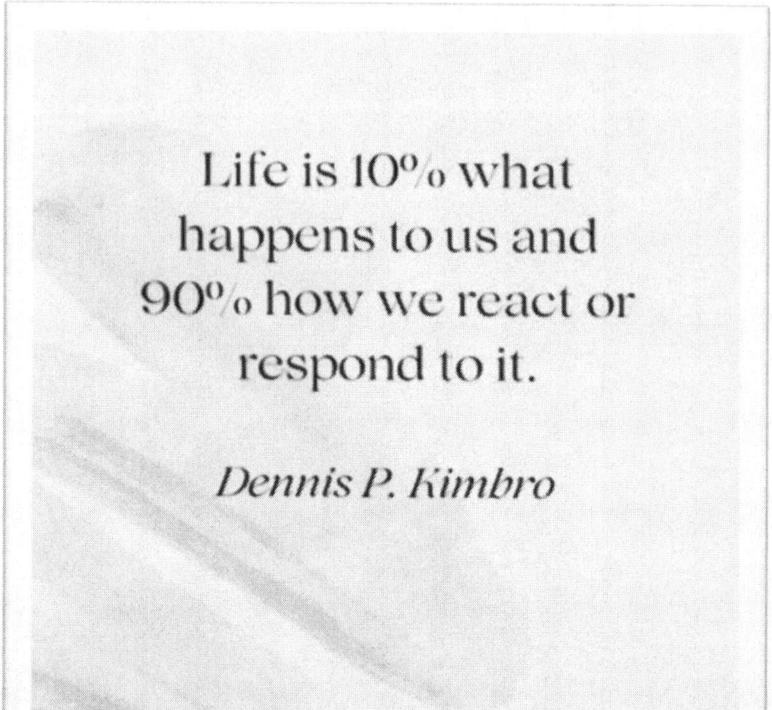
Life is 10% what happens to us and 90% how we react or respond to it.
Dennis P. Kimbro

CHAPTER 13

The Law of Requisite Variety

Now, I realise that this may sound a little scary. What the heck is this law, and why is it appropriate in the context of *Clearing my Head to Get Ahead and building resilience*? To put it a little more simply, the Law of Requisite Variety, which came from the mind of Robert Dilts, states that the person or system with the most flexibility of behaviour will control the system.

What?

The more flexible you can be, the more control you will have.

There…that's better…or maybe not. According to systems theory, our bodies, our societies, and our universe form an ecology of complex systems and sub-systems, all of which interact with and mutually influence each other. That's to say, we are all interconnected. I think it's safe to say now that we mostly believe we are just forms of energy and that if we were close enough, your energetic field would influence mine and the other way round, and so it's not possible to completely isolate any part of the system from the rest of the system.

If you are still with me, it means that all the interactions that take place within a human being and between human beings and their environment follow certain basic principles and rules of systems. Biological and social systems, for instance, are based on certain 'self-organising' principles and naturally seek optimal states of balance or homeostasis.

The Law of Requisite Variety states that to successfully adapt, achieve or survive, a member of such a system requires a minimum amount of flexibility. That amount of flexibility has to be proportional to the variety that members must contend with in the rest of the system.

So, what has this got to do with managing stress and being in your best state possible to be at your best? Well, imagine you are a taxi driver (maybe you are) and you have to get your passenger across town to the airport. The passenger calculated it's just a 20-minute drive and so left himself just 20 minutes, BUT there's been an accident. If you had just one way to get across town and were not flexible in your route, the temperature inside your taxi would be getting a little hot as your passenger realises that there's not enough time left to get to the airport to catch the last flight home.

However, imagine now that you are better than that and have done your homework. You know several routes from where you are to the airport and even a couple of secret ones that, while they may take a little longer on a "normal" day, today is far from normal. You use your incredible database of knowledge to whisk your passenger across town, and he makes his plane as planned. Unfortunately, you've done such a good job he didn't realise there was a problem…but that's not the point.

The point is with your flexibility of behaviour, you controlled the system and not the other way round.

Your world is what
you think it is, but
there's a world
beyond your thinking

Michael Neill

CHAPTER 14

Decision Fatigue

Have you experienced decision fatigue? I'm sure you have; you may just not have had a word for it. It's that feeling when you get toward the end of a busy and even stressful day, and you simply can't make another decision. You can't figure out what you should cook for dinner, and even the idea of picking something to watch on Netflix seems like a chore. You are suffering from decision fatigue.

We all experience these days, and the more taxing your job is the more you're required to make decisions throughout the day, and the more you find yourself suffering from decision fatigue. This shouldn't come as a big surprise. When we spend all day walking or running around, we feel tired in the evening and our muscles are fatigued. If you've ever participated in an endurance sports event or gone for a long run after a period of inactivity, you've experienced muscle fatigue. Why shouldn't we experience the same when we tax our minds with lots of decision making?

Not only does decision fatigue impair our ability to make decisions altogether, but it also affects both the quality of our decision making and our willpower. In short, after a long day of making good choice after good choice, we tend to start making bad ones. There's a reason we see a lot of "made for TV" products and infomercials on TV late at night, and it isn't just because of the cheaper advertising rates. It's because that's the time of day we're most prone to making impulse purchases. It's also when we give up on our diets and healthy eating intentions.

Keep this idea of decision fatigue in mind when you try to get a few last-minute tasks done at the end of a long day. That may not be the best time for important choices or jobs that require well thought out responses or clear decision-making.

Similarly, you should expect your team members, co-workers, bosses, and loved ones to experience the same. Asking your boss for a raise right before quitting time on Friday may not be a good idea. Your chances of getting a "yes" significantly increase if you wait until first thing Monday morning. Don't expect your family to make healthy dinner and snack choices in the evening; instead, plan your meals early in the day and have them figured out well before lunchtime.

Important Lesson #1 – Don't tackle important or difficult decisions late in the day, particularly if you've already made a lot of decisions in the hours leading up to it.

How To Cut Daily Decisions From Your Life

Now that we've established that there is such a thing as decision fatigue, we'll investigate some things we can do to avoid it. The answer is simple. We need to find a way to reduce the number of daily decisions we make. Here are some simple ideas for cutting some of them from our lives.

Use Habits and Routines to Your Advantage

Let's start with something you already know how to do; you may just not realise it. That's creating routines and habits to cut back on the decisions you must make. You don't have to decide to brush your teeth every morning or talk yourself into deciding to go to work today. Instead, they are habits and things you do without thinking about them and, more importantly, without having to waste any of your precious limited decisions.

As you go about your day and make decisions, particularly if they are decisions that you regularly make, stop yourself and see if there's a way you can turn that decision into a habit or routine.

Instead of spending the first minutes of your day figuring out what you should wear, create a simple uniform. Find a few pairs of similar trousers and a couple of mix-and-match tops. Rotate through those outfits, so you always know what to wear on a given morning.

If you have a recurring task at work, schedule to do it first thing in the morning or right before you head to lunch. That gets it out of the way without having to decide when to take care of it.

Another great solution is to batch your decisions and plan ahead. Let's use your food choices as an example. We all eat, and we make quite a few daily decisions about what to eat. You can cut those out of your daily routine by creating a weekly or monthly meal plan. Start with dinner. Sit down and come up with your dinner ideas for the week. Write them down and post them on the fridge door. When you go grocery shopping be sure to pick up everything you need. That way, you don't have to agonise about what to fix for dinner when you get home after a long day at the office. From there, expand and include breakfast and lunch plans. You can even choose a daily snack for yourself. For bonus points, create a couple of these menus and start rotating through them weekly. Once you've made your original meal plans, there's no more decision making involved.

You can easily adapt this principle to other areas of your life and work. Sit down and make out a to-do list first thing in the morning or before you head home in the afternoon. You can batch a whole bunch of decisions together and have a game plan for your workday. Think about other ways to incorporate this into your life and cut back on the decisions you make.

Delegate And Cut Down Choices

Last but not least, start reducing the choices you have to make altogether. Not every decision has to be made by you. If you're working in a team or have people under you, don't be afraid to delegate. Yes, in the beginning, it's a little extra work to explain what needs to happen and what's involved, but as you start to delegate and give these people more and more responsibility, your decision-making tasks will be considerably cut back. This allows you to focus on critical stuff.

Another great strategy is to simply cut down on the number of choices you give yourself and others. Get in the habit of trimming the list before you even attempt to choose.

These tips may seem like little things, but they will quickly add up. It doesn't take a lot of decision cutting-back to notice a big difference in when and how hard decision fatigue hits. Give it a try.

Good News – Decision Making Ability Replenishes

I thought we should end on a high note. The good news is that your decision-making abilities replenish, and they do so regularly. In the last section of this short report, we'll visit the various ways we can encourage that replenishment and when and how it happens naturally. In general, your decision-making ability replenishes with rest and relaxation. Since we're getting less and less of that in these busy times, it's no wonder decision fatigue is becoming a big issue.

Decision-Making Ability Replenishes Overnight

Don't panic when you find yourself unable to make another decision at the end of a long day. Overnight, sleeping replenishes your ability to make smart choices. You'll be back to a clear head and able to make important decisions in the morning. Use this to your advantage. If you feel decision fatigue is setting in, rein things in for the rest of the day, don't schedule important meetings in the evening and use your mornings wisely.

Sometimes It Pays to Take a Mental Health Day

We all get busy, and we all get stressed out sometimes. When a good night's sleep doesn't seem quite enough to bring your decision-making batteries back to full strength, it may be a good idea to take the day off. Do something fun, relaxing, destressing, and most significantly, make as few decisions as possible and certainly no important decisions. You'll come back refreshed and ready to go.

Go Outside and Get Some Air

Sometimes taking the day off or waiting for the next morning isn't an option. An important decision is expected from you before you leave the office or within the next hour or so. If you feel decision fatigue is setting in when a decision is needed there are two things I want you to remember. First, all other decisions can wait. Focus on making just the one more that can't wait.

Second, go outside, get some air, and clear your head before you make your choice. While this won't work as well as sleep or a day off, it may be just enough to give you that little boost of energy and willpower you need to make the right decision.

It May Be Time for a Holiday?

Finally, let's talk about taking a few days off and going on holiday. You know from experience how invigorating and restful a trip can be. Take advantage of this and come back ready to make those important decisions about the future of your company, your family, or the projects you want to tackle during the next quarter.

Above all, use your decision-making skills wisely and learn to recognise decision fatigue before it leads you to make bad choices.

Resistance is the first step to change

Louise Hay

CHAPTER 15

Insomnia and Sleep

This is a long chapter. Readers are warned they may fall asleep before reaching the end. Maybe that's the intention.

Have you ever suffered from insomnia? Do you face difficulty falling asleep and staying asleep at night? So, what causes it?

Often, insomnia is caused by multiple reasons, like not getting enough rest, hunger, psychological trauma, and so on. No matter the reason, millions of human beings suffer from the devil called insomnia. It robs you of enough rest, saps your energy and destroys your productivity the next day. Not to mention the detrimental effect on your physical and mental health.

First, are you suffering from insomnia or external disturbances? Insomnia is difficulty falling asleep and staying asleep. It is the type of restlessness a person suffers at different points of their sleep cycle. A simple indication to diagnose insomnia is when a person is not satisfied with the amount of sleep they are getting.

Those with insomnia will feel a lack of energy, fatigue at different moments of the day, difficulty in concentrating on tasks, terrible mood disturbances and having a low-performance level in the workplace. It's possible for insomniacs to have any of these symptoms after staying awake throughout the night.

A human body requires rest to rejuvenate both mind and body. A lack of rest in either of these will result in fatigue and various mental illnesses. Although they are utterly exhausted to the core, insomniacs still fail to fall asleep or stay asleep for various reasons. Without being able to fully recharge, we cannot be at our best for the new day, and not being at our best leads to mistakes and less than optimal decisions.

There are two main types of insomnia. The first is the kind when you only suffer a couple of restless nights. Often, you're able to fall asleep and stay asleep easily. Many insomniacs might not think that they are suffering from it, but the fact is, they could be having acute insomnia. This kind of insomnia comes from the core levels of stress that insomniacs are experiencing at that moment. They will face a short period when they are not able to fall asleep because of their life circumstances. This type of insomnia doesn't last for a prolonged time and happens because of certain factors or events during a specified period.

For instance, acute insomnia might occur after insomniacs face the wrath of their boss, get a bad grade on a test, are rejected by their crush, or merely because they're having a 'bad day'. These situations can cause a person to have a night or two where they simply cannot get any sleep. Many people may have experienced this kind of insomnia and it tends to resolve on its own.

The second type of insomnia is chronic insomnia. This occurs at least three nights a week and lasts for at least three months. Usually, it occurs when someone is facing a significant change in their environment, either physically or mentally. It could bc moving to a new home, losing a loved one, being in a new workplace, facing challenges in school, or having problems adapting to harsher weather. Chronic insomniacs may have trouble sleeping because they have an unhealthy sleep habit without a proper sleep routine.

It's common in today's world; modern society has screwed up our sleep cycles with shorter hours of sleep. To make things worse, many people sleep at odd hours; they don't practice the habit of going to bed early and rising early the next day.

As a result, the mind doesn't know when to shut down and becomes accustomed to staying up late. That's why insomnia has become a common problem today. What people fail to understand is that the body will not function well with a small amount of sleep one night and expect to compensate for the sleep gap by taking naps during the day. While this may seem possible and useful in the beginning, this sleep pattern is not sustainable in the long term.

Eventually, the mind and body will collapse, and you will experience complete exhaustion until you get enough rest. The best solution is to have a fixed schedule for sleep and practise a healthy sleep routine; otherwise, you need to visit the doctor for medication. Typically, it will be linked to another medical or psychiatric issue, meaning that you have chronic insomnia due to stress. What seems to be a typical situation will seem stressful if you have chronic insomnia. A restless mind and body will feel annoyed by any stimulus from the immediate environment.

The Causes of Insomnia

Regardless of the types of insomnia, the causes are the same. The difference lies in the intensity of emotions a person experiences for a set amount of time. Underlying medical conditions can also cause insomnia. Fortunately, insomnia is treatable in most cases. These medical conditions can be either severe or mild, inducing insomnia to occur at a different point in a person's life. These conditions include nasal allergies, sinus allergies, lower back pain, overall chronic pain, gastrointestinal problems, arthritis, asthma, and other neurological problems.

The stress on the patient's body will cause the mind to stay awake for a longer period. For instance, those who catch a cold will realise that they are staying awake for most of the night, or they might find themselves waking up frequently. Both these factors can result in a person having a severe lack of sleep and rest. They might try to relax while having a cold, but insomnia will prevail.

Physical pain can also cause insomnia as the body cannot get into a comfortable position to rest. Have you ever experienced sleepless nights because you're unable to get into a comfortable position? This situation is typical when you experience any pain in your body. The best way to fall asleep and stay asleep fast is to get your body in a comfortable position in bed. This will also aid in healing and ensure a more productive sleep. Otherwise, you'll find yourself in a constant battle to fall asleep and may even opt for unnecessary medication if you can't get into your best sleeping posture.

With all these different causes in mind, we can now move on to the cure. But it's just as important to study all the factors that cause insomnia. Did you know insomnia carries risk factors? If you find some of these risks apply to you, then you have a higher chance of having insomnia at some point in your life. Otherwise, pay attention to your health and sleep habits to make sure that you are insomnia-free for the rest of your life.

The Risk Factors of Insomnia

The risk factors of insomnia include being female, being pregnant or in the period of menopause, being an adult over the age of forty, suffering from extra stress, suffering from depression, having a night-time job, travelling long distances with a time change, and have a family history of insomnia. All these factors lead a person closer to insomnia, but do you realise that most of these risk factors are the results of your choices? People often think they have little to no choice in life, but this is not true.

One can choose to take a longer vacation when moving through different time zones but doesn't. One can go for a day job but decides to go through the hard times of a night job while adapting to an entirely different lifestyle.

It is hard to deal with the risk factors of insomnia, but ultimately, it all depends on your choices. Sometimes, you may go through tough times in life, including relationship, family, or job problems. Not only that, but you might also be suffering from financial or personal problems with trouble balancing your professional and personal lives. All these will beat you up and keep you up at night until most of the stress or depression is gone. In some cases, it might take longer. In other cases, people can find solutions and get through the tough times rather quickly. Either way, having the right mindset is the cure to emotion-induced insomnia.

Since insomnia has many different causes and risk factors, you can do a variety of things to prevent yourself from having more sleepless and restless nights. Most of the time, it's easy to find out what the causes are, but the real challenge is how to overcome the problem and have a good night's sleep. Life can be difficult, and sometimes it can beat a person down to the point where they are not even sure if they can get back up.

The very first step in overcoming insomnia is to be fearless. Do not be scared of any outcomes or results that might or might not happen. Fear introduces more stress into your life that doesn't serve you. In fact, it can only intensify your insomnia. Prevention is always better than cure. Always remember to stay calm and follow correct health tips to prevent yourself from having insomnia.

The Brain of an Insomniac

Researchers all around the world are putting their minds together to figure out how the brain of an insomniac works. They continue to look towards the features of the brainwaves and how thoughts interact during the day and night.

At every hour of the day, the mind can adapt itself to any new situation. Whether you're trying to get food, get a drink, get out of a car, walk through a door, or just get some rest, the mind will constantly try to find new ways to survive and flourish. It will continue through the cycle of getting enough resources during the day and having enough energy to heal and rest during the night.

Normally, people with a healthy level of brainwaves with satisfactory cognitive stability during the day can shut down parts of their brain's thought process during the night. As night falls deeper, the brain will begin to slow down and initiate sleep. Alertness and focus typically decrease when it's nighttime. This is why many people find it harder to complete tasks at night.

Studies show that the mind's process will naturally change throughout the day and can sometimes cause a major form of anxiety. This is when the brainwaves become erratic and refuse to slow down due to an immense amount of stress experienced during the day. The mind will not be able to relax completely at night and instead will go through a period when the brain waves move unusually fast, causing more thoughts and consuming more energy in the evening. Everything that a person has been through during the day will be recollected at night. The body will then run through twice the amount of energy and resources to process the thoughts, and this causes fatigue and lack of energy the following day.

As for the mind and how brainwaves respond to the phases of insomnia, there are three different studies to show how the brain reacts during the night. It has been proven that the brain's learning and memory processing functions affect a person's sleep. The more you learn during the day, the more thoughts and memories will be processed by the brain during the night.

Dreams come from one's thoughts and real-life experiences. The more you experience in life, the more you dream at night. The ability to have a greater variety of dreams allows the mind to calm down and form vague images to reinforce your memory. When you fall into a deep slumber, you tend to be in the dream state. Sometimes, you might even have nightmares. But it all boils down to your subconscious thoughts and the kind of experiences you had.

Day vs Night

So, what's happening in the brain of insomniacs? First, their brain is more active during the night and has difficulty reaching a calm and relaxed state. In one of the studies on brain waves during insomnia, scientists have proven that the neurons of insomniacs' brains are more active at night.

Insomniacs tend to have a lot of thoughts going through their head which results in insomnia. They experience a constant state of information processing throughout the entire day without the ability to put a stop to it. Ultimately, they'll have insomnia and face the consequences of not getting enough rest.

Experts claim that insomnia should not be seen directly as a night-time disorder. In fact, it's more of a 24-hour brain condition that causes the brain to remain active throughout the day.

Sleep plays a major role in processing and storing memories. A lack of sleep will interfere with your memory in the long run. You'll have trouble concentrating and remembering facts and even minor details. This theory was tested out with a group of students on a short test. One group had a full night's sleep while the other group didn't have any sleep the night before. The results? The students who had more sleep were able to focus more and could recall their answers a few hours after the test. The students who didn't have enough sleep struggled with the test, scored below average, and could hardly recall the answers they wrote an hour after the test!

The Myths

The goal of this experiment is to prove the importance of rest to focus and memory. As a matter of fact, insomniacs can't have the same level of concentration as those who had enough rest. Surprisingly, some people believe that they can have the same attention span during the day. Just because a brain is as active at night as it is during the day doesn't mean the brain can function at a peak level.

Brain plasticity is the ability of the brain to change structurally and functionally in response to physical or environmental factors. Besides the lack of concentration, research shows that insomniacs have more brain plasticity; however, research on how plasticity contributes to the states of insomnia is still unknown. What is known is that the brain's plasticity builds up throughout a person's life and contributes to other forms of disease later.

In most cases, brain plasticity enables us to absorb new information, learn new things, and continue to grow throughout adulthood. But insomnia damages your brain cells and leads to brain plasticity, which in turn leads to poor memory retention and lack of focus, not only on a short-term basis but also in the long-term. It becomes more challenging to hold onto all levels of concentration and memory when a person grows older.

The Brain of The Restless Mind

Another research was done to find out how stress and anxiety affect sleep. The goal was to determine whether a person with a stressful lifestyle has insomnia and how the brain responds at night, and here's the result: The cognitive function of the brain doesn't change regardless of someone having insomnia; however, insomniacs find it more challenging to focus and process information throughout the day.

Most research shows that insomniacs' minds wander during the night. They will have difficulty concentrating the next day and will face challenges in managing their work, studies, and even their personal lives.

In other words, the mind will find it difficult to function optimally the day after lacking sleep and insomniacs are unable to perform at their best. Another part of the research compared the memory function and the efficiency of completing tasks given to both insomniacs and those who had enough rest.

Studies show that insomniacs cannot recall most of their memories during the day. As a result, they face difficulty in completing their daily tasks. Their minds wander even when they're performing simple tasks. For example, when it comes to preparing breakfast, those with a healthy amount of sleep will go to the kitchen, make quick choices, and start their day. Conversely, insomniacs will enter the kitchen, open several cabinets, look through the same foods, and be unable to figure out what they should have for breakfast!

And here's the explanation: An insomniac's brain waves are slower, and this will cause them to move at a slower pace and forget simple things quickly. Furthermore, as they go through the day and as more tasks come their way, their prefrontal cortex will begin to have fewer resources, and the brainwaves will become erratic. The brain will try to stay active, but it won't have enough energy to process everything. Therefore, the brain will eventually exhaust itself if you're suffering from insomnia.

The Grey Matter

The third and final scientific study is to determine the role of the brain's grey matter. The most important thing to know about grey matter is that it exists in the frontal lobe and controls the processes of memory and executive function. When insomniacs don't get enough sleep at night, they will have a substantial decrease in grey matter. Whether they are suffering from insomnia or having trouble sleeping overall, they will slowly start to develop symptoms of depression or trauma. Usually, the underlying cause of insomnia is stress. The best way to resolve this issue is to consult a doctor to find out what kind of medicine would be best for you.

In a nutshell, the mind must gain enough sleep and rest to have adequate concentration. Insomnia will only put your body into overdrive mode and thus deprive it of enough rest. The next important thing to remember is to get enough nutrition and sleep every night. No matter how difficult it is to find a balance, it is important to have a high level of concentration every day to get the most out of your day.

Sleep-starved - The Devil

So, we've explored the mind and now understand how insomnia directly affects the brain. Having this disorder for any amount of time will cause a massive negative impact on the mind. Besides memory loss, insomnia also results in tiredness, carelessness, and lack of alertness the next day. The mind and body both need rest to function well the next day. If there is no rest, the grey matter, memory, and elaborate duties of the mind will crumble and insomniacs will have a difficult time getting through the day. Their mind will wander, and they will struggle to stay focused.

The Five Things You Do Every Morning

Here's a little exercise: Reflect on the first five things you did the moment you woke up today Perhaps you turned off your alarm clock, checked your phone, stood up, switched on the lights, and walked to the bathroom. No matter what your usual routine is, you tend to execute your regular activities flawlessly. Believe it or not, you subconsciously perform all these actions without giving them much thought because they have become a daily routine.

However, when you have insomnia, you are not nearly as focused as normal. The mind will continue to think as quickly as usual, but it does not have all the resources and energy to function properly. In order words, you may find it difficult to perform your first five activities in the morning and struggle to complete each task.

An easy way to recognise this is if these tasks took longer than they should. The five actions that usually take only two minutes to complete might end up taking more than ten minutes when you don't have enough rest. You might even forget to do a task or two. You might forget to turn off the alarm, or you might forget to check your phone for updates. Many different things can happen, but overall, this is the tip of the iceberg when you are struggling with insomnia.

Damaging Your Professional Life

After the first night facing insomnia, you might notice a significant drop in your energy level. It may be difficult to plan the day, or you might find it more challenging to remember all the information you need.

In most cases, your daily routine may begin with waking up, getting ready for work, and maybe shopping afterwards. All jobs require 100% focus to ensure high performance and efficiency, otherwise, you may face the music from your boss. No matter how exhausted you feel, you will only be given sympathy for a limited number of days. There are only so many sick leaves you can take in a year. So don't let insomnia destroy your personal and professional lives. Take charge and get rid of it once and for all.

In your job, you are doubtless expected to complete tasks before a certain deadline. Whether you pack boxes, do research, or write, you have to be at the top of your game almost every day. You must perform at your best all the time and earn your well-deserved pay cheque at the end of the month. Any rest sacrificed during the night can result in poor performance the next day.

Are You Experiencing Sleep Starvation?

Everyone has their unique sleep rhythm and experts recommend six to eight hours of sleep daily. The exact number depends on the individual. Some of us need more rest, some less, but at the end of the day, losing a couple of hours sleep is always better than losing a whole night of rest. For instance, instead of getting eight hours of sleep you only get six. Those two missed hours may seem crucial, but they will not do as much damage to your life as insomnia. Losing two hours of sleep may slow you down, but the chances are you will still be able to pull it through and get all your tasks done by the end of the day. On the other hand, losing an entire night of sleep can shut your brain down and you will go through the day struggling with simple tasks.

For instance, when your boss puts an agenda on your desk you can read the content without a problem, but the tricky part for those with insomnia is understanding what each item on the list means; what seems to be a walk in the park may seem like mission impossible.

Often, you lose focus and purpose for the day if you lack sleep. You are constantly looking for the fastest way to get through the day rather than considering the best way. In the beginning, it might seem manageable because you're still able to get things done on time occasionally. But the truth is, it'll hurt your reputation in your workplace in the long run because of the poor quality of your work. Also, insomniacs are known to have bad tempers and poor working relationships with their colleagues.

People will notice your inefficiency eventually. Your boss will realise that you are working at a slower rate, that you are not focusing as much, and that you do not have the right attitude to complete the job. This can put you in the wrong favour of your boss, and you might risk being fired. Although this may seem unlikely to you right now, you should keep in mind that the possibility is very high. Insomnia is a distressing element of life that can not only cause someone trouble in the workplace but also in their personal life.

Damaging Your Personal Life

When you think about your personal life, think about all the things that are important to you, things you hold dearly to your heart. You might think about your wife, husband, children, pets, or any other elements. Some people might even think about their garden or the remodelling project they have been working on.

There is no right or wrong answer to this. It's your life and the key to success in your personal life is to maintain balance. Most people perform their daily routines without putting much thought into them. Examples are simple tasks such as preparing breakfast for your kids, getting into your car, or going somewhere to eat.

Normally, these aren't difficult tasks, but an insomniac might feel otherwise. The moment a person's personal life starts to veer off balance stress appears and they begin to question if there is any way to get back to a steady state. It doesn't matter if the stress is coming from not having the groceries in time or waking up late, minimal amounts of stress can accumulate into something out of control. Insomnia causes significant levels of stress and exhaustion.

There won't be any specific thoughts in their mind, it will only wander with random thoughts without context. The same can also be applied to their work life. If you are suffering from insomnia and you need to prepare your kids for school, you might miss the lunch box or forget to iron their clothes etc.

Always remember to put yourself first as "Self-Love is NOT Selfish". When you constantly put yourself last, you'll find yourself in a downward spiral, unable to fulfil your ultimate purpose in life.

Now is the time to blow the lid off a huge misconception in our society, the perception of putting yourself first as being arrogant, evil, and selfish. If you're busy fulfilling the demands of others while not achieving your life purposes, you'll feel unfulfilled and doomed. You'll lose your drive, motivation, enthusiasm, and productivity if you journey down this path. So, stop pleasing others and prioritise yourself first. Only by doing so will you have unstoppable momentum to accomplish more and have more to offer in return.

At home, you might need to mow the lawn or walk around the house to check for bugs. No matter what you do, remember the steps to execute each action accurately. The moment you are suffering from insomnia, you will not be able to remember things very well, and you will have a harder time getting them done.

Another vital part of your personal life is your relationship with others. Whether it's your partner, husband, wife, boyfriend, or girlfriend, being in a relationship is a job on its own. If you fail to pay full attention to your partner because you didn't have enough rest, you can expect your relationship to go sour. This situation will lead to arguments, dissatisfaction, frustration, loneliness, and sadness in a relationship. All these emotions can go awry to the point where major confrontations might need to take place.

Dealing With Insomnia

It's hard to deal with insomnia when you have no energy left inside you. You'll feel tired all the time and care little about things happening around you. Your mind will wander, and your thoughts often don't make any sense. Life is already hard enough.

Now, imagine adding in the factor that you are not getting any rest and must deal with every obstacle life presents you. How would you feel? Overwhelmed? Stressed?

You might end up wasting time at your workplace. You might fail to prepare your family meals and upset your children. You might start forgetting about all the little things that you usually do for your romantic relationship. Many areas in your life can go south due to insomnia. With all these in mind, now is the time to protect yourself from losing sleep and get optimal rest every night.

The Cure: Natural and Artificial Options

Sleep is incredibly important for health. We need sleep for our bodies to heal and rejuvenate from our day's activities. Unfortunately, many people either have difficulty falling asleep or simply don't get enough sleep, which is where insomnia remedies come in, and there are two basic categories.

1. Artificial Remedy

The first are the artificial remedies which can be found in pharmacies and clinics. They are mostly prescribed to target the sickness at source and usually cost a bomb, but typically deliver fast results. Most medicines today are toxic and filled with harmful chemicals that are not safe to be consumed for a prolonged period.

2. Natural Remedy

The second are natural Remedies. People have practised natural medicine for centuries and this type of remedy utilises the body's natural healing process for beating insomnia. They are often less expensive, but what makes them stand out is the fact that they're not as toxic as artificial remedies.

Regardless of which kind of remedy you choose, the goal is to help you fall asleep and stay asleep. Most of these remedies will cause drowsiness, so it's best to take them right before bed unless it states otherwise.

It is important to get a medical evaluation before you take sleeping pills. Visit a doctor for a thorough examination. Always consult your doctor about the adverse effects of any medication before deciding which pills to take. Each drug can cause different side effects. The side effects can be a headache, a severe allergic reaction, or prolonged drowsiness to just name a few.

Some prefer to go for natural remedies. You don't have to depend on chemicals with harmful adverse effects, especially upon waking up. Instead, why not use natural remedies to repair your sleep cycle and put an end to insomnia? This is my personal recommendation. While the pharmaceutical industry has helped me have the health I have today I'm doing my best to be free of my prescription medication. To truly have that *clear head.*

So, what are your options?

1. Go Camping

When the lure of the TV or scrolling on the phone keeps you up late at night, it's time to grab the tent and go camping. Stay away from electronic devices and enjoy a digital detox occasionally. Put yourself in a distraction-free zone and be mindful of your surroundings and yourself.

Utilise this time to meditate, do some yoga, write, recollect your thoughts, or simply breathe.

According to several studies, campers who stay away from gadgets and practice winding down rituals such as meditating or listening to music fall asleep about two hours earlier than usual.

Digital devices contribute to insomnia, and it is found that artificial light sources can negatively affect circadian rhythms.

Try sleeping on the ground, not in your car or a cabin. That way, you'll get grounded and be one with nature. Regardless of what you do during camping, the goal is to relax, remove yourself from distractions and demands from others, stay away from artificial light, and be one with nature. Bathe under the natural sunlight and fall asleep when the sun goes down. In no time at all you'll reset your sleep rhythms.

2. Use Music Therapy

Music has been used since ancient times to combat insomnia. It is a healing tool that can help ease anxiety which can contribute to poor sleep quality. The major advantage of this technique is that it's easy to use and has no side effects.

There are many different types of music therapies, and they differ in the types of neurological stimulation they evoke. For instance, classical music can be a powerful tool for comfort and relaxation while rock music may cause discomfort. Try to go for soft relaxing music that includes sounds of nature like the ocean, birds, a waterfall, etc.

Several studies showed that people who listen to calming music before going to bed have more improved sleep quality during the night than people who don't. Hence, if you're having trouble falling asleep, this could be a solution.

3. Power Down For Better Sleep

Sleep is not an on-and-off switch. Your body needs time to unwind and ready itself for shuteye. Insomniacs often find it difficult to shut off their brain at night. You can try to power down for better sleep. This technique aids in quieting things down so that your body will understand it's time to get some rest. To set the stage for sleep, it is vital to unwind and dim our mind.

For instance, a warm bath before bedtime will drop your body temperature, triggering the body to start prepping for sleep. By taking a warm shower, your body temperature will slow down metabolic functions like breathing, digestion, and heart rate. Your body will understand that it's time to slow down and relax. If you listen to music before heading to bed every night, your body will be conditioned that listening to music at night signals bedtime.

It's all about habits and conditioning. Carve out at least half an hour of wind-down time before bed to do breathing or relaxation exercises to clear your mind. The goal of this power-down hour is to signal your brain that it's time to wind down, relax, and sleep.

4. Sleep In A Cool Room

People facing problems falling asleep usually have a higher core body temperature immediately prior to going to bed when compared with their healthier counterparts. Thus, this group of insomniacs needs to wait at least two to four hours before their body temperature lowers and brings on sleep.

Research shows that the optimal room temperature for sleep is between 16 and 20 degrees Celsius. When you're trying to sleep, your brain enjoys the cold environment.

Besides, sleeping in a cold bedroom also helps with anti-ageing, releasing anti-ageing hormones known as melatonin, a potent antioxidant that tackles inflammation, strengthens the immune system, and prevents cognitive deterioration and cancer.

There's a saying that those who go to bed early and rise early live longer. It makes a lot of sense considering that sleeping in a cold bedroom reduces neurodegeneration and oxidative stress. I could go on and on regarding the anti-ageing benefits of having a good night's sleep in a cold environment.

Insufficient sleep delivers a lot of harmful effects to your physical and mental health. Ultimately, it can put your life at risk. Make sure you fix your sleeping habits and begin doing so by creating an optimal sleeping environment by lowering the bedroom temperature.

5. Break A Sweat

Exercise early. It's no secret that exercise improves sleep and overall health, but a study published in the journal *Sleep* shows that the amount of exercise done and when make a difference. Researchers found that women who exercise at a moderate intensity for at least 30 minutes each morning, seven days a week, have less trouble sleeping than women who exercise less or later in the day. Morning exercise seems to positively affect our body rhythms that in turn improves our sleep quality, and it's what I do. You don't need to join a gym. Gyms provide some social interaction that we do need, but you can work out and get amazing results just by doing your workouts at home with very little to no equipment. To see an example of how this works I use and recommend the YouTube channel for The Body Coach, Joe Wicks. Give it a go, but as always, if you are new to doing physical exercise take it easy to start with. Check with your general practitioner if at all concerned.

One of the reasons for this interplay between exercise and sleep may be body temperature. Your body temperature rises during exercise and takes up to six hours to drop back down to normal. Cooler body temperatures link to better sleep, so it's important to give your body time to cool down before bed.

Sleep is a crucial part of our health and healing. Take it seriously and seek out the help of a functional medicine practitioner if you can't get your sleep under control. All these require discipline and commitment. Once you reset your biological clock and fall back into a normal sleep rhythm, you'll finally enjoy the benefits of restful, restorative sleep.

Lifestyle Modification for Insomniacs

Previously, we talked about the two fundamental categories of remedies to overcome insomnia. However, these extrinsic factors cannot deal with the root causes of insomnia. Yes, you can feel better after trying these remedies, but insomnia can only be healed completely if the origin of the problem is removed. Otherwise, there is a high chance that insomnia will return.

So, what is at the root of insomnia? For many, the primary cause of insomnia is having a poor lifestyle and sleep habits. Simple lifestyle changes can make a world of difference to the quality of your sleep.

Although not all insomnia is caused by stress, it is undeniable that people who experience ongoing stress are more susceptible to insomnia. In the case of stress-related insomnia, treating or eliminating the stress will alleviate the insomnia. As mentioned earlier, stress affects the quality of one's sleep which can upset one's sleep rhythm. Thus, one will find it difficult to fall asleep at night and stay awake during the day.

It is important to handle all parts of your life in the best manner possible to ensure that you are at a healthy balance. You need to get sufficient sleep daily. Sleep plays a major role in your physical health. Insufficient sleep for a short time may make you moodier and more irritable but the long-term effects can be serious, including cardiac problems, depression, stroke, and heart attack.

According to sleep experts, several studies show that when people get sufficient sleep, they will not only feel better but will also increase their odds of living longer, healthier, and more accomplished lives.

To overcome insomnia, you should stay away from nicotine, caffeine, and alcohol. All these will cause the mind to become restless. Continually topping up with caffeine will force the mind to be more active than it would be.

Most people need energy to start their day, so they choose a stimulant. Caffeine is one of the most popular choices of stimulants today to ensure alertness and wakefulness in the morning and for the rest of the day. However, people are ignorant of the fact that caffeine is one of the leading causes of insomnia. It screws up the natural balance of wakefulness and sleep.

Therefore, insomniacs should stay away from these drinks to have a quality sleep. Skip that coffee break, reach for a glass of plain water instead. The coffee may be the reason you are having trouble falling and staying asleep at night.

Besides that, setting up a sleep schedule is one of the best self-help techniques for insomnia. It is a major step in overcoming insomnia for good. It is so important to go to bed at the same time at night and wake up at the same time every morning because the body needs consistency. The body likes a routine; it thrives on habit. With a regular bedtime and wake-up time, your body is more likely to stay on track. If you can, avoid alternating schedules, late-night parties, night shifts, or other things that may disrupt your sleep schedule.

When you have a difficult time falling asleep, try to drink a glass of warm milk. It is a traditional remedy for insomnia, and there's evidence that it can help you to get better quality sleep. Not only does milk help prevent hunger from disturbing your sleep, but it also contains an amino acid called tryptophan, which is converted in the brain into a "relaxing" chemical known as serotonin. Calcium is very pro-metabolic, reducing stress and decreasing levels of the parathyroid hormone which has been known to play a role in insomnia.

You can adjust your daily schedule to include time for yoga or meditation. There is an abundance of evidence that yoga and meditation can improve sleep patterns, often dramatically. Having some relaxation time for yourself is important. These techniques can be done at home for both comfort and privacy. It helps to increase the total flexibility of your body, relax your mind, and destress your body. Try to spend at least 30 minutes a day to either meditate or do yoga. Typically, meditation and yoga are best done in the early morning, in a quiet place, with exposure to sunlight.

For meditation, all you must do is sit down and clear your mind. Try to listen to relaxing music to help calm you down. The moment you start to get used to the idea of meditating throughout the day, your mind will be able to relax faster at night and therefore you will have an easier time falling asleep.

As for yoga, you can either go to yoga classes with a bunch of friends or practice at home for more privacy. It will benefit your sleep in many ways. The practice of certain yoga postures increases the blood circulation to the sleep centre in the brain, which has the effect of normalising the sleep cycle.

Remember, sleep is not a lifestyle choice or a luxury; it is natural and necessary. Root out the underlying causes, change your diet, drink a glass of warm milk, set up a sleeping schedule, do some yoga, and meditate. Follow the advice mentioned above and eventually, you'll get your quality sleep.

Switching Off

Battling Insomnia

Fighting insomnia is an uphill battle. When you are trying to cure insomnia, you are trying to stop your mind from being too active at night. There is no reason to be afraid of staying up for countless nights in a row and wondering if it is all going to end.

Worrying will only bring more sleepless nights. So, stop battling insomnia in your head! All you need to do is 'Switch Off' your monkey brain.

At night, you want your mind to slow down to the point where you can quickly fall asleep. Having a proper amount of sleep helps you to stay fully alert the next day and ensures a good night's rest. One reason people struggle to fall asleep is that their monkey brain refuses to shut down. Often, they start thinking about useless things that serve no purpose but only hinder them from falling asleep.

Switching off needs practice. For many busy adults, the only time they reflect upon their lives is at bedtime! It's good to reflect occasionally, but not at bedtime. This is often the worst culprit that stops you from falling asleep.

For those who want to reflect on their lives, consider waking up earlier to have time in the morning or even schedule some time in the evening to do some reflection.

Stimulating Night = Bad Sleep

Another reason why people fail to switch off is they have many over-stimulating activities at night causing them to stay awake instead of feeling tired. Some even love to drink caffeine at night! No wonder people are struggling to fall asleep! Stay away from coffee, your mobile phone, laptop, and television at bedtime. Avoid activities that force you to think and require physical exertion at night. And most importantly, avoid the blue screen from electronic devices.

Never Miss Another Night of Sleep

Another key to falling asleep is to schedule your sleep. Most people don't do that. Instead, they choose to fall asleep only when they're tired. What you should do is set up a routine and schedule your bedtime. By acting on repetitions, your mind will be conditioned to switch off when the clock hits the usual hour to fall asleep.

Having a regular sleep routine is arguably the best technique to ensure a better quality sleep. In fact, our bodies thrive on consistent sleep schedules and regularity. Although there's no one-size-fits-all solution, having a consistent sleep routine will definitely help in beating chronic insomnia once and for all.

How To 'Switch Off' At Night

The first thing you should do after you have eaten dinner and cleaned up for the night is turn off your electronic devices. Having your phone or computer switched on when you are getting ready for bed will stimulate your brain and eventually hinder your sleep. Admit it, your electronic devices are addictive, and you won't know when to stop.

The light will interfere with your sleep pattern and cause you to stay wide awake. It's recommended to avoid using your gadgets at all costs at least one hour before bedtime.

Reading before sleep is fine, but not through an electronic device. Reading a physical book before bed actually helps you in getting ready to sleep, but it's better not to read in your bedroom. I encourage you to read in another room since you do not want your mind to be active in the room in which you need to fall asleep, again, to condition your mind to switch off the moment you step into your bedroom. If you can completely relax when reading a book, it's fine to do it while laying down in bed, otherwise it's best to read in another room.

The next thing you can do is listen to music and write down any reminders you need for the next day. The music will help you to calm your mind and remove your stress. Try to listen to music that is smooth and slow in rhythm. Listening to anything loud or exciting will stimulate your mind and it will be harder for you to fall asleep. For instance, you'll find yourself in a much more relaxed state when you listen to classical music than rock music.

Another tip is to plan your day ahead before sleeping. Writing down reminders for the next day helps clear out your mind. Staying awake in bed while constantly reminding yourself that you need to remember something will keep your mind active. Think of your notepad as a "dump it and forget it" vault. Simply grab a piece of paper and scribble a few notes down. It will help you calm down and fall asleep faster.

You can also have a relaxation drink such as tea right before bed, however, make sure you stay away from caffeine, alcohol, and drinks with lots of sugar. A nice cup of herbal tea can calm your mind and help your body relax.

This is also an excellent way to create time for yourself; a time to quiet down and relax. You can do this while either reading or listening to music. If you don't find pleasure in drinking tea, then consider having a light snack before bed. Do not consume anything that is too high in calories and difficult to digest. Regardless, a light snack is good because sometimes the reason why you're having trouble getting to sleep is simply due to hunger.

Another way to ensure restful sleep is to bring down your room temperature. The best way to do this is to set your bedroom thermostat to be a bit cooler. Our body is conditioned in a way that when it enters a cooler environment, it will get a signal that it's time to rest.

Also, why not take a quick shower right before bed. Preferably a cold shower to immediately cool down. Otherwise, you can try to get a bed fan, a cooler mattress, or go for a short walk before bed.

All the things listed above can be a part of your bedtime routine. Go ahead and try them out and figure what works best for you and your schedule. In no time at all, you won't have any trouble falling asleep and staying asleep again.

You are, of course, free to try any tips and strategies listed in this book to ensure a restful sleep. After all, restful sleep is the foundation for your mental and physical well-being. Whether it's an artificial or natural remedy, lifestyle changes, or setting up a routine, all contribute to preventing insomnia.

What next? It's time to act… today!

Find out which of these methods works best for you and implement them into your daily routine. Write them down and imagine how your average day looks when you add these strategies to your routine.

Only by trying them out can you find out the best way for you to overcome insomnia.

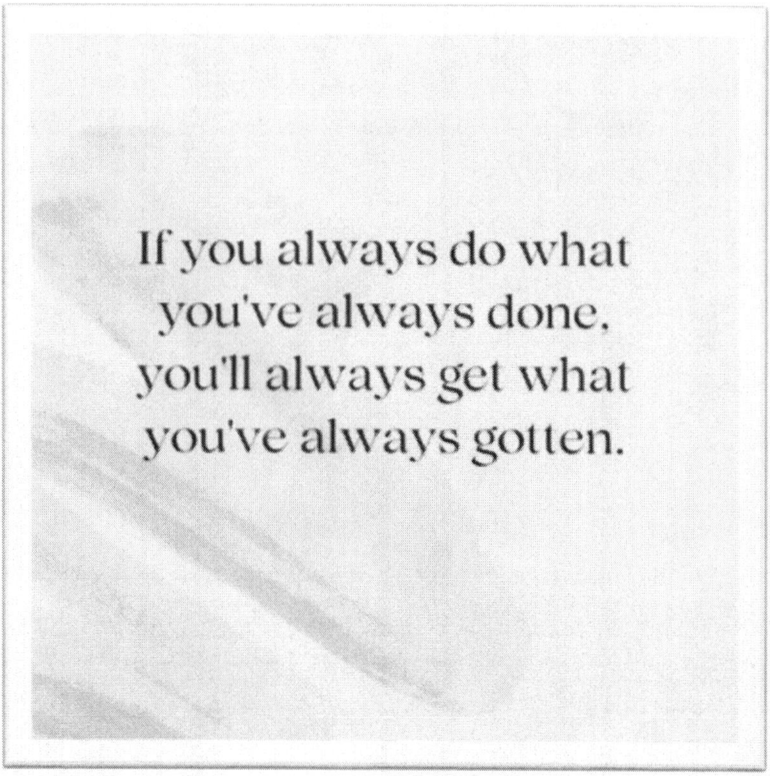
If you always do what
you've always done,
you'll always get what
you've always gotten.

CHAPTER 16

Lifestyle Alterations

There's an old saying, sometimes attributed to Albert Einstein, sometimes to Henry Ford or even Tony Robbins, that states something like, "if you always do what you've always done, you'll always get what you've always got." In other words, at some point you need to do something differently, or even something completely different, to achieve what you want to achieve.

In this case, if you come into this book, read it, and leave, then without doubt your mindset, clarity of thought, quality of sleep, and ability to handle stress and become more resilient just won't happen. I haven't spoken with a single person in private practice who cannot acknowledge that if they go back to what brought them here, even after a full recovery, they are likely to relapse and suffer further burnout. Something must change.

This chapter is a kind of round-up where you could just do what's in here and find some improvements in your life, but it would be a shame as you'd be missing out on so much more inside the rest of the book.

You can do a lot by following the experience of others outlined in this book and some of the hints and tips you've read along the way, but however beneficial private practice is, your environment might also need looking at, especially the workplace culture.

Kurt Lewin, the German-American psychologist, understood this back in 1936 when he published his equation B=f(P,E). Interesting, isn't it! It states that an individual's behaviour (B) is a function (f) of the person (P), including their history, personality, and motivation, and their environment (E), that includes both their physical and social surroundings. So, given that most people's history, personality, and motivation change little, your behaviour mostly reflects the environment you are in. For the most part this directly comes down to where you work, or more specifically who you work for; how you are treated at work, how the boss treats you etc. If your environment is triggering your stress and adding to your stress load then, according to that saying above, you're still going to get stressed.

There are five fundamental ways you can ease the stress in your life and they're all based on simple modifications you can make in your own lifestyle. From better planning to diet and exercise, even better sleep, you can take control of the situation and feel better in an instant.

Eliminate and Modify Your Plans

Sometimes, we put ourselves directly in the path of oncoming stress. The first thing you must do is become aware.

Awareness is key to managing stress loads, and sometimes we turn a blind eye to things that upset us the most. Get yourself a journal and jot down an entire week's worth of stress. Whenever you feel upset, even if it's only for 20 minutes, write down the root cause and how long it lasted.

Once you become aware of repeating factors in your stress load, you can work to eliminate or modify how you interact with them on a regular basis, if at all!

Traffic is a good example of stress, and some people fight traffic day after day, both during a morning commute and early evening rush hour. You can improve the situation to some degree, like leaving earlier for work or taking a different route. Of course, there will also be times when you will be stuck, so make plans now about what you might do if you are. I find that just the simple and powerful act of breathing while focusing on something or someone that brings me joy can make traffic jams more than tolerable.

Romantic relationships can cause a great deal of stress when they become less romantic and more volatile. Instead of hanging onto something toxic in your life, address it head on, perhaps with couples counselling or by breaking it off and opening your life up to something healthier for you. Having had my fair share of breakups I firmly believe that the moment you realise it's not right is the best time to share that decision. Let's face it, it's nearly always going to hurt, but the longer you leave it, the deeper the pain. Be brave enough to "nip it in the bud".

Familial relationships are sometimes toxic, too. Some people can't close the door on family, but you can learn how to construct safe boundaries by not allowing yourself to be used or abused.

Friendships can be unhealthy and stressful. Know when to have a talk with a friend about the way you're being treated and when to let go of these friendships that do more harm than good.

Finances are a major source of stress, and many people

think they're powerless to control them, but they're wrong. You can pursue a good debt management strategy and pay off what you owe, start saving and begin earning more if you plan for it.

Control Stress By Controlling Your Diet

Stress affects our diets and digestion in many ways, and stress is affected by our diets, too. Most people only grasp the unhealthy connection, i.e. comfort eating during periods of high stress.

The first thing you need to do is stop emotionally soothing yourself with food. Then, look at ways that food can become your friend during times of stress. What we normally do when comfort eating is binge on high salt and high sugar foods. Look for foods that have an opposite effect on your body than stress does. For example, stress causes you to feel fatigued, so in the past, you might have turned to sugar to get a jolt of energy.

Nuts are a great food that instantly go to work in your body to keep cortisol levels down when they spike. Cortisol is the stress hormone that gives you that "fight or flight" feeling when anxiety hits.

High potassium foods like bananas and avocados help combat stress. When you get stressed out, your blood pressure spikes. Foods rich in potassium help lower your blood pressure.

Another thing that happens when your body feels stressed is your blood sugar can spike. Some foods, like oatmeal or whole-grain breads (complex carbs), stabilise your blood sugar and help keep you calm. They also boost your serotonin (feel good) hormones. Certain foods filled with folic acid help keep stress low. Any dark, leafy green like kale, collards, spinach, or turnip will work. Citrus foods, beans, and seeds will also do the job. One of the health side effects of chronic stress is constipation. If this affects you, turn to foods high in fibre. Beans, corn, whole wheat foods, oatmeal, and berries are all high in fibre, and make sure you keep hydrated; drink your water!

Researchers have discovered that those who lack vitamin B have a propensity to develop feelings of anxiety. You might be lacking in this, so eat foods rich in B vitamins like shellfish, soy, low-fat dairy, and eggs.

Let Your Endorphins Snuff Out Stress for Good

It's a myth to think that if you exercise, all your stress will simply disappear. It doesn't work like that. While movement has been shown to quickly reduce the levels of cortisol in your bloodstream, stress will be around you no matter what. What exercise does is help you be better able to handle stress so it doesn't take the same toll on you that it is doing today.

Endorphins are commonly called happy hormones because they create a "feel good" effect in your mind when they hit. They are actually neurotransmitters that get released in your body to fight the cortisol (negative hormone) that's bringing you down.

Many people form a love of exercise because after a while of engaging in it, they become used to the endorphin release. Not only does it deliver physical stress relief, but it also clears your mind because it allows more oxygen to reach your bloodstream.

At first, you might feel tired from exercising, but over time, exercise helps you feel less fatigued. You'll become stronger, have more energy, and your mental clarity will skyrocket.

When you exercise regularly, you end up seeing long-term stress-relief benefits. Not only will your mood improve but you'll also sleep better at night. Getting enough exercise is great, but even a quick five-minute aerobic jolt to your system can pack a punch when it comes to endorphins.

One way to get more exercise is to have fun with it. Don't make it a chore. If you hate going to the gym, then don't! Do something else instead, like rollerblading or another activity or sport that gets your heart rate up.

It's not just aerobics that release endorphins. Even slower exercise has that effect, just at a different level. You can engage in meditation or yoga and feel the benefits of endorphins being released.

Exercising also delivers other health benefits to your body, like assisting you in managing your blood pressure, for example. When stress hits you and your blood pressure rises slightly, exercise will already have you at more manageable levels, so you won't be putting yourself in danger.

If you have been sedentary for a long period, it's best not to jump right into a strenuous routine where you might possibly harm or injure your body from the rigorous movements.

Start out slower and in small increments and build on your routine from there. As you increase your time and effort, you'll start to feel even more of the physical and mental boost that you get from engaging in this form of stress relief.

Improve Your Sleep and Watch Stress Dissipate

If there's one thing that creates a vicious cycle in the stress world, it's insomnia. The sleep and stress cycle is brutal because if you don't get enough sleep, you get stressed the next day, and if you're stressed, you can't sleep.

Where does it all end?

It ends when you regain control of the situation. It's one thing to address the stress that you can deal with, but you also have to handle the sleep issue on its own.

It's almost a chicken and egg situation. Nobody knows which came first, the insomnia or the stress, but you must tackle it head on to make sure it gets sorted out.

Start by making sure you have good sleep hygiene. That means a comfortable bed with clean bedding, set your room temperature to a nice, cool level, and remove all technology from the room to help induce sleep.

Develop a bedtime routine. This trains your subconscious mind to know when it's nearing bedtime and it starts to shut down and feel drowsy. That might mean taking a nice, warm bath, reading a book, or having a light snack to stave off hunger until morning.

If you're easily woken up during the night and then find it hard to fall back asleep, make sure you help yourself not get roused from your slumber. That might mean using a white noise machine so that you don't hear sounds easily.

You can buy a white noise machine that's meant to drown out noise, or you can use things like a fan in your room, turned to a setting that hides outside noise from you.

You might need something to help you drift off. In that case, try aromatherapy. It can be dispensed in the room with scents like lavender that has a soothing aroma to relax and calm the mind.

Sometimes it's nothing you're doing, but something your sleeping partner is doing that makes you unable to sleep. If you have a partner who has sleep apnoea, for example, they need to get fitted for a sleep apnoea mask so that they're not choking themselves awake and startling you in the middle of the night.

You may need to use an over-the-counter helper like melatonin, which weakens as you age, to help you fall (and stay) asleep. You can start with a low dose and increase it until you find one that works best for you.

Indulge in Self Care to Tame Terrible Stress

Sometimes our minds just won't quit. They relive the day's stress even when we're out of immediate danger. If this happens to you, you'll need to work on specific nurturing to your body and mind to help alleviate the pressure your mind is putting on you.

Everyone has a different idea of what self-care means. For some, it includes a little much-needed "me time" away from everyone; time to just be alone with your thoughts and free of distractions.

You might find that taking time for a nice, warm bath each night is plenty of relaxation for you. Or maybe you need to get out of the house and engage in an activity like photography, sports, or socialisation.

Sometimes we need a little more specific self-care. You might save up for a stress-relieving spa activity like a manicure, pedicure, massage, or facial that will relax you.

You can also do all those things yourself at home using organic skincare products and essential oil blends that promote relaxation in your home. There are many spa tools for at-home use that might help make it a wonderful experience.

You may need to engage in some serious mental stress relief. For example, you can meditate or use guided meditation if you don't know how to do it on your own.

You may also want to check out how EFT (Emotional Freedom Technique) works. This is a tool you can use anywhere discreetly to provide instant stress relief.

There are many ways you can help control stress in your life. And for the stress that you're unable to avoid, you can always educate yourself about how to better manage your reaction to that stress.

Sample the ideas and try combining those that work best for you. Sometimes, a specific stress relief tactic won't deliver results for you, and that's OK. It just means your body and mind will react to a different strategy better!

About the Author

Before running the successful Coaching and Training business Inspire Coaching GmbH in Basel, I profited from nearly 30 years in global corporate organisations, mostly in the pharmaceutical sector, including BioTech. Starting in sales and then marketing, I moved into internal communications in 1998.

This was a move away from the hustle and bustle of sales and marketing into one that gave me deeper insights into other areas of the business like R&D, late-stage chemical development, and global supply.

My first foray into the coaching world started with the Gallup StrengthsFinder assessment which had a profound effect on my life. I realised that I really was in the wrong job. I got so much more energy from the informal coaching that I had been doing and the report from Gallup spelt that out. So, when the opportunity presented itself, I retrained as a psychological coach and started my own coaching practice.

Since then, my studies have helped me understand emotional intelligence (RocheMartin), and I became the first Gallup-certified strengths coach in Switzerland.

In 2012, I became an NLP Master Coach and in 2014, a Certified Trainer and Coach Trainer for NLP too, and now run NLP certification courses for others at the Centre for NLP. My most recent, and potentially most fascinating, tool for use with clients is the Integrative Enneagram.

These days, my coaching is far-reaching as I help my clients gain their own deeper insights into what stops them from getting what they want. Anything from getting on board a plane to landing their dream job or promotion and particularly moving people, teams, and organisations from stress to strength as well as getting to the root cause of their stress and anxiety and learning from it in a way that helps build their resilience.

Outside of work Martin is married to Carol, his biggest fan and supporter, and with whom he runs Inspire Coaching GmbH in Basel. He has two children, two stepchildren and, at the time of publication, two amazing grandsons and a step granddaughter, all of whom are a source of wonder, amazement, and inspiration.

For more information you can find Martin on LinkedIn, Facebook, and Instagram and through the websites for Inspire Coaching GmbH and his own website Martin-Daubney.com. Should you get to any one of these, please do stop and say hello.

Or, better yet, book your complimentary call right here, right now by scanning the QR code below.

Scan and book your call.

The Last Page

You can copy this page or you can rip it out and scan it and have multiple copies. Use it as a reminder to have a break, or pause ... (or two paws).

Made in the USA
Middletown, DE
08 October 2022

12230608R00104